PLEASE RETURN THIS ITEM
BY THE DUE DATE TO ANY
TULSA CITY-COUNTY LIBRARY.

FINES ARE 5¢ PER DAY; A
MAXIMUM OF $1.00 PER ITEM.

rsa CS

FEB    1989

D1480099

DUE DATE

FEB 15 1989

# Wolfpack

# Wolfpack

## Hunting MiGs over Vietnam

## Jerry Scutts

*Motorbooks International*
Publishers & Wholesalers Inc.
Osceola, Wisconsin 54020, USA ®

This edition first published in 1988 by Motorbooks International Publishers & Wholesalers Inc, PO Box 2, 729 Prospect Avenue, Osceola, WI 54020 USA.

© Jerry Scutts 1988, first published by Airlife Publishing Ltd., Shrewsbury, England, in 1988.

All rights reserved. With the exception of quoting brief passages for the purposes of review no part of this publication may be reproduced without prior written permission from the publisher.

Motorbooks International is a certified trademark, registered with the United States Patent Office.

Printed and bound in England by Livesey Ltd., Shrewsbury.

The information in this book is true and complete to the best of our knowledge. All recommendations are made without any guarantee on the part of the author or publisher, who also disclaim any liability incurred in connection with the use of this data or specific details.

Library of Congress Cataloging-in-Publication Data
Scutts, Jerry,
    Wolfpack : hunting MiGs over Vietnam/Jerry Scutts.
       p.   cm.
    ISBN 0-87938-281-3
    1. Vietnamese Conflict, 1961-1975—Regimental histories.
2. United States. Air Force. Tactical Fighter Wing. 8th—History.
3. Vietnamese Conflict, 1961-1975—Aerial operations, American.
4. MIG (Fighter planes)  I. Title.  II. Title: Wolf Pack.
DS558.8.S38 1987                                                    87-34893
959,704′348—dc19                                                    CIP

ISBN 0-87938-281-3

Motorbooks International books are also available at discounts in bulk quantity for industrial or sales-promotional use. For details write to Special Sales Manager at the publisher's address.

959.704348 S437w 1988
Scutts, Jerry.
Wolfpack :

# Contents

TULSA CITY-COUNTY LIBRARY

# Introduction

In World War 2 the unofficial title 'Wolfpack' belonged to the 56th Fighter Group assigned to the 8th Air Force in England. Led for most of its existence by the brilliant tactician Hubert Zemke the group was the first to receive the Republic P-47 Thunderbolt in the US before leaving for England in January 1943. Unique in retaining the Thunderbolt when the rest of the 8th's fighter groups re-equipped with Mustangs, the 56th ended the war with more aerial victories than any other Army Air Force group in the European theatre — 647.5.

While the evocative and highly appropriate unit title was to be resurrected the number of the unit which would make it famous over Vietnam had been around since April 1931. On the first of that month the 8th Fighter Group was activated at Langley Field, Virginia. By May 1942 the unit had become the 8th Fighter Group and was part of the 5th Air Force in Australia. Weathering the difficult early period of operations against the Japanese, the 8th initially flew P-39 Airacobras, P-40 Warhawks and P-47s. In the spring of 1944 all three squadrons converted to the P-38 Lightning and by the end of the war the 8th FG had destroyed 443 enemy aircraft.

Based in Japan with the Far East Air Forces the unit became the 8th Fighter Wing in August 1948 by which time it was flying the P-51 Mustang. By 1950 jet equipment had arrived in the shape of the F-80 Shooting Star, and as the 8th Fighter-Bomber Wing the unit was one of the first to see action in Korea. After a brief return to using the F-51 the 8th FBW was back with the F-80 by December 1950, having established itself in Korea some two months previously. Advancing Communist forces obliged a return to Japan and the wing was not based on Korean soil again until June 1951. During the course of the war the 8th FBW chalked up an impressive record, primarily in support of United Nations ground forces. On 22 November 1952 Maj Charles J. Loring Jnr was awarded the Medal of Honor for deliberately diving his badly damaged F-80 onto a Communist gun position threatening the rest of his flight.

When the USAF sent fighter squadrons to Korea to counter the threat posed by the MiG-15, it was the 4th Wing, the 56th's old rivals in WW2, which took the lion's share of the victories, but there was no longer an outfit calling itself the Wolfpack. After the end of the Korean war in 1953, the 8th Wing remained in Japan with F-86 Sabres, the type with which it had re-equipped in April 1953, some three months before hostilities ceased.

The F-100 Super Sabre came along in 1956 and the 8th Wing maintained a quick reaction strike force as part of the defence of Japan. On 1 July 1958 the unit became the 8th Tactical Fighter Wing. In 1961 the wing operated the F-102 alongside the F-100s and the 8th became an F-105 Thunderchief operator in 1963, although Delta Daggers were retained until 1964.

On 13 May 1964 the wing's tactical squadrons were detached and on 18 June all components except headquarters were inactivated. The 8th Wing moved without personnel or equipment to California, absorbing the resources of the 32nd TFW. With the arrival of the F-4 Phantom the wing spent a year or so in training, exercises, operational readiness inspections and so forth, prior to its move to Thailand in December 1965.

Some hard times lay ahead; the wing's motto 'Attaquez et Conquerez' would however, not be in any way humbled by the Vietnam experience. Just as the 8th Pursuit Group had from 6 September 1934 set out to 'Attack and Conquer' so too would the F-4 equipped 8th TFW make both the unit number and the name Wolfpack synonymous once more with a top-scoring fighter wing.

# Chapter 1
# Unreal war

The McDonnell Douglas F-4 Phantom officially entered service with the United States Air Force on 20 November 1963, following a ceremony at McDill Air Force Base near Tampa, Florida. Ordering an existing Navy aircraft for the Air Force was seen as an interim move pending the first flight of a new strike fighter to replace the Republic F-105 Thunderchief, then under study as the TFX programme.

Phantoms would provide a rapid bolstering of Tactical Air Command's strike capability at a time when the Thunderchief was nearing the end of production and service entry of TFX was still some years in the future.

The enormous potential of the US Navy's F-4B over anything TAC then had in inventory, could hardly have failed to impress even hard-bitten Air Force chiefs who had not previously considered ordering a Navy aircraft.

The Phantom's all-round performance (Mach 1.5 at 40,000 ft/12,192 m) and load carrying capability (maximum 10,000 lb/4,536 kg) coupled with the cost-effectiveness of a minimum modification programme to tailor the F-4B to land-based operational requirements, made the McDonnell fighter particularly attractive. As things were to turn out with TFX, the decision to acquire Phantoms was indeed fortunate.

In March 1962 the USAF issued a Military Interdepartmental Purchase Request (MIPR) for the F-4 to the manufacturer via the Navy, which acted as intermediary. Evaluation of the aircraft was made with F-4Bs loaned by the Navy, followed by inspection of a mock-up of a production-configured Air Force model, the F-4C. On 18 September 1962 US military aircraft designations were revised and the original F-110A designation allocated under current USAF nomenclature was subsequently dropped, as was the provisional name 'Spectre'.

Changes made by McAir to the F-4B airframe included replacement of the General Electric J79-7 engines with J79-15s, each of 10,000 lb (4,536 kg) thrust, incorporation of a self-contained cartridge/pneumatic starter that did not require an externally-coupled air hose as on the Navy machine, and relocation of the 20 kVa alternator for each engine from a waist location to a bullet-shaped fairing under the extreme nose. This cone housed an infra-red seeker on Navy F-4Bs and retention of its fairing was an example of the USAF's policy of not changing the Phantom any more than was absolutely necessary.

Known as the F-110A Spectre until designations were revised in 1962, F-4B BuNo *49405* was the first loaned by the Navy for evaluation that spring. Carrying a variety of stores, this aircraft was given temporary USAF 'buzz numbers' and branch of service identifiers, but a clue to its actual ownership is the forward position of the national insignia, it being Air Force practice to paint this on the aft fuselage. *(MDC)*

Flight refuelling equipment was modified to enable a tanker boom to plug into a receptacle aft of the cockpit and use a fuel transfer system generally favoured by the USAF over the Navy- preferred probe and drogue method. Wider-section wheels and tyres were specified, Navy mainwheels being considered too narrow with tyres that were too hard for use on Air Force asphalt runways. The new wheels for the F-4C had 11.5-in (292 mm) hubs as against the F-4B's 7.7-in (196 mm) hubs, necessitating the most noticeable external change on the first (and all subsequent) Air Force F-4s, a wing root bulge to accommodate the wider wheels in their bays. Wider hubs also allowed the fitting of anti-skid brakes.

Other changes made to the F-4C included full dual controls as a standard fit; the rear cockpit instrument panel was lowered about three inches (76 mm) and control consoles installed on each side of the rear seat. Improvements in the second cockpit were the result of USAF crewing requirements for its Phantoms: at the time the aircraft entered service there were to be two rated pilots, the front seater being the Aircraft Commander with a Pilot/Systems Operator occupying the rear, whereas a Navy F-4 crew comprised a Pilot and a non-pilot-qualified Radar Intercept Officer. Later the Air Force would adopt a similar crew complement.

A Litton ASN-48 inertial navigation system replaced the navigation computer fitted in the F-4B and an AJB-7 all altitude bombing control system and LADD timer were added; the radar was updated by installing the AN/APQ-100 without increasing the scanner diameter of 36 inches (91 cm). An AN/ANS-46 navigation computer was also added.

These revisions under Specific Operational Requirement (SOR)-200, extended the Phantom's already diverse weapons delivery capability, enabling it to use air-to-ground missiles such as the GAM-83B Bullpup, which required a command-guidance box in the rear cockpit. Primary air-to-air weaponry remained similar to that of the F-4B — the radar-guided AIM-7 Sparrow, four of which were carried semi-recessed in the belly of the aircraft, and the AIM-9 Sidewinder heat-seeker AAM. While no provision was made for fixed gun armament, Air Force Phantoms were tested with GUU-17 Vulcan guns in streamlined pods carried on fuselage centreline or wing hardpoints.

The first production F-4C *(62-12199)* made its maiden flight on 27 May 1963, by which time Air Force crews had already conducted numerous training flights using borrowed Navy F-4Bs. Thirty examples were acquired to initiate training at McDill, the first two, complete with TAC badges and Air Force 'serials' based on the Navy Bureau of Aeronautics numbers, being delivered to TAC on 24 January 1962.

Co-located at McDill were the two wings which would introduce the Phantom to Air Force service, the 12th and 15th. The former unit received its first F-4Cs in January 1964 and was fully equipped by July. The 12th TFW was declared operationally ready by October, some two months before its component 555th Tactical Fighter Squadron deployed for duty to Kadena AB, Okinawa.

Primary armament of the F-4 wings in SE Asia was the AIM-7 Sparrow AAM, seen here prior to loading by USAF ordnancemen, circa 1966. *(USAF)*

Flight line scene at MacDill AFB, Florida, with at least 29 new F-4Cs in residence. Tactical Air Command markings of the early 1960s made few concessions to unit identity and aircraft of both the 12th and 15th Wings are believed to be shown. *(MDC)*

As the Phantom began to enter service with the USAF, America had already experienced the start of one of the most traumatic decades in its history. The terrible events in Dallas on 22 November 1963 were all too fresh in the memory and the new man in the White House had inherited an unenviably long list of potential challenges to US interests around the world: there was Cuba; the increasing strength of China; Russia, also with a new and as yet unquantifiable leader — and there was Vietnam.

Lyndon Johnson was faced with a far from clear set of policy decisions over US involvement in South-East Asia. There was no doubt that the situation there was deteriorating as the North Vietnamese-backed Viet Cong stepped up its campaign of guerrilla war against the government of the South. Johnson sought, through Maxwell Taylor, US ambassador in Saigon, what was widely regarded as a prerequisite for any further US military assistance, namely political stability of the South Vietnamese government.

Acutely conscious of the possibility of massive Chinese intervention in Vietnam (with its obvious parallels with Korea) if the US either committed combat troops in strength or unleashed its airpower to devastate North Vietnam, Johnson hesitated. His National Security Council had drawn up a list of 94 prime targets which, if attacked in a short, all out series of air strikes, would very likely significantly reduce the flow of supplies and men sustaining Viet Cong military operations in the South.

Also bearing in mind retaliatory attacks on US dependants in the area, Johnson chose what seemed to be a less risky option — he authorised a 'slow squeeze' series of air attacks on enemy infiltration routes through Laos. This course avoided any worldwide condemnation of US 'aggression' in a war that had not yet reached major proportions.

An attack by North Vietnamese naval units on elements of the US Sixth Fleet in the Gulf of Tonkin on 2 August 1964 gave Johnson the option to carry out reprisal attacks on North Vietnam. Later that year Viet Cong success in the field and the bombing of the Brink Hotel in Saigon forced Ambassador Taylor to re-assess his belief that stability in the South should precede air strikes on the North. He instead recommended immediate reprisal. This was vetoed by Johnson on 29 December and things deteriorated further in the early part of 1965; further Viet Cong attacks on US installations were made on 7 February and the government of General Nyugen Kahn fell on 18 February, to be replaced by that of Dr Phan Huy Quat, who would hold office for only four months. Quat returned power to the military and a new regime led by Nguyen Cao Ky emerged on 24 June.

Johnson had little choice but to show a firm American response; on 19 February B-57s flew the first overt USAF strike mission of the war and authorisation was given for Flaming Dart and Rolling Thunder air strikes on Laos and North Vietnam — but only as far as the 17th parallel of latitude, an area a few miles above the demilitarised zone dividing the two Vietnams. It was still Johnson's belief that Ho Chi Minh could be persuaded to negotiate a cease-fire without widespread air attacks on his territory.

While there began an expansion of US airpower strength in South Vietnam to undertake ground attack and support missions in conjunction with government forces, the bombing of North Vietnam would be better served by using South-East Asia Collective Defence Treaty Organisation (SEATO) bases in Thailand. As a SEATO signatory and recipient of US military assistance, Thailand had a number of air bases which could accommodate USAF strike squadrons; although conditions were often primitive by US standards, these bases were — unlike those in South Vietnam — all but immune to attack by guerrillas.

A more subtle change in markings occurred when the first F-4s went to South East Asia in 1964, buzz numbers generally being painted out as shown on this F-4C *64-730* (and no doubt the one behind it) parked ready for action in Thailand. F-105s are much in evidence in the background.
*(USAF)*

Should North Vietnam attempt to attack US bases in Thailand, the Royal Thai Air Force, equipped as it was with well-maintained, if obsolescent F-86 Sabres, would be able to provide at least a token defence. Additional defence was provided by USAF F-102s at Don Muang Airport outside Bangkok.

By February 1965 the USAF had 83 aircraft based in Thailand, the majority of them being F-105 Thunderchiefs based at Udorn and Takhli, along with a small number of support types, including rescue helicopters. The strike aircraft flew sorties into Laos under the direction of the 831st Air Division of Tactical Air Command which itself was subordinated to the 13th Air Force, one of two USAF air command components of Pacific Air Forces. With the 7th Air Force controlling USAF operations in South Vietnam, the 13th had headquarters at Clark AB in the Philippines and encompassed three fighter and two reconnaissance wings, plus support groups which would operate from RTAF bases for the duration of the SE Asian commitment. Each Air Force had a joint command link for the planning and conduct of 'in country' (South Vietnam) and 'out country' (North Vietnam) operations.

As the US buildup continued (the first eight F-105s had arrived at Korat on 9 August 1964, these being machines of the 36th TFS which staged from Yokota, Japan, to Clark and thence to Thailand), reconnaissance sorties showed that the North Vietnamese were taking steps to counter any future air strikes on their homeland. Photographs taken on 7 August revealed 39 MiG-15 and -17 fighters at Phuc Yen near Hanoi, but plans to conduct a strike aimed at eliminating this threat were shelved.

With each passing week in which the US did not send its bombers into the North, there was a gradual but definite increase in the country's defences, to the extent that when Rolling Thunder operations did begin on 2 March 1965, the enemy was well prepared. The bombing 'pauses', whereby the US carried out a number of air strikes and then to all intents and purposes sat back and waited for reaction from the North, started even before Rolling Thunder began. After only the second (Flaming Dart I) strike by the Navy on 7 February 1965, four days elapsed before Flaming Dart II was flown on 11 February. The reaction was nil and the terminology changed. Flaming Dart became Rolling Thunder.

North Vietnamese response to the new round of air strikes was equally non-apparent, and when all interested parties had been consulted, from the US President down to the ambassadors in Saigon, Vientiane and Bangkok, further sorties by the F-105s went ahead. Under the highly complex 'rules of engagement', US aircraft based in Thailand could attack targets only in Laos and North Vietnam — not the South. General Joseph H. Moore, commanding the 2nd Air Division at that time, in effect received his orders direct from the Oval Office.

Johnson's personal target selection was passed through Defence Secretary Robert McNamara to the Joint Chiefs, who in turn issued strike directives to Commander in Chief, Pacific (CINCPAC), where targets were shared out between the Air Force, the Navy and the SVNAF. When target strike authorisation was finally 'fragged' to the air bases they carried a concurrent list of restrictions and precautions designed on the one hand to minimise North Vietnamese civilian casualties and ensure that the right targets were struck with

If anyone doubted the Phantom's naval origins Air Force F-4Cs made it pretty obvious through their grey and white colour scheme, which gave way to camouflage in 1966. (MDC)

the ordnance estimated to render a repeat strike unnecessary; on the other hand they appeared to do very little to minimise casualties among US aircrew from heavy enemy defences.

Increasing the number of US strike aircraft in Thailand meant instigating a parallel programme of improving and expanding existing RTAF bases and building new ones. The USAF progressively used seven main bases in Thailand, at Udorn, Nakhon Phanom, Takhli, Korat, Ubon, Don Muang and U-Tapao, the first five being those primarily concerned with strike operations. Takhli, Korat and Ubon were located on a line roughly across the centre of the country, with Udorn and Nakhon Phanom the two most forward, up near the border with Laos. Don Muang and U-Tapao were furthest from North Vietnam, the former adjacent to Bangkok and the latter near the coast on the Gulf of Thailand.

The Thai climate is invariably hot or rainy with high humidity levels often pushing temperatures above the average 85°C from late March to May or June. This is the hottest period of the year in central Thailand — a country which really has only two seasons. It is hot from February to September and rainy from October to January. Rain can fall from June to October but thereafter the weather is generally much more pleasant; daytime temperatures are high although the nights are cooler with much lower humidity.

Into such conditions came sophisticated aircraft tasked with an exacting operational requirement, packed with equipment, particularly electronics that could be expected to react adversely to this environment. Inevitably there were problems but the F-105, which had not exactly enjoyed a trouble free service period at home, stood up to the rigours of combat far better than expected. A high humidity level with attendant difficulty in keeping moisture away was the major cause of equipment malfunction and the damp atmosphere was to have some effect on certain components used on the F-4.

7

The Thai bases lay about 350 nautical miles from the urban centres of North Vietnam, clustered around which were the industrial plants which constituted the main strategic targets. But there were precious few of these. US Intelligence reckoned that there were nine main ones — comprising steel rolling mills, cement plants, hydroelectric power sources, rail marshalling yards and the largest bridges in a country criss-crossed with waterways. To more positively identify the targets written in reports and verbal debriefing of pilots, North Vietnam was divided into six regions known as Route Packages, the lowest (Roman) numeral being used for the most southerly area. As the numbers rose to VI, the threat

Boom operator's view of an F-4 taking on fuel. KC-135 tankers were indispensable to sustaining the air war.

Gradually a little colour crept back into an otherwise dull camouflage scheme — witness the drop tank decoration on these F-4Cs. The red lion marking appeared on both grey and camouflaged F-4s. *(USAF)*

increased proportionately — Route Pack VIA and VIB took in Hanoi and Haiphong. One reason for introducing such jargon was the often tortuous spelling and pronunciation of North Vietnamese place names.

Not only did presidential advisors fix the targets to be attacked, but they also chose the routes which US air strikes should follow on ingress and egress. With ordnance also selected many miles from the operational airfields there was little else for field commanders to do if their orders were to be followed 'to the letter'. The restraints did perhaps minimise possible casualties amongst the civilian population of North Vietnam, yet inevitably, bombs fell short or overshot their relatively small targets. It was not surprising, given the strength the defences were allowed to build up to. Funnelling air strikes down narrow corridors, denying American pilots the right to self-defence attacks on airfields and gun sites, telling them in no uncertain terms not to overfly 'sensitive' areas of North Vietnamese territory, the US went to war over North Vietnam. It tried at the same time to assure the world at large of its best intentions and that its main object was peace in Vietnam — indeed there is every reason to conclude that such a policy was believed, certainly by Lyndon Johnson.

After the 19 March start of USAF Rolling Thunder operations, strike sorties were conducted on a weekly basis, targets being limited primarily to radar installations and road and rail bridges between the 17th and 19th parallels. Strikes just above the DMZ had limited early escort from F-100 Super Sabres and F-104 Starfighters, both types also flying some ground attack missions. B-57 Canberras were part of early Rolling Thunder operations although the intense flak surrounding most important targets soon forced all but the F-105 and the B-52

Russian-made SA-2 Guideline surface-to-air missiles posed a significant threat to US strike forces — although their actual effectiveness was largely overcome by superior ECM tactics developed by the US. Here a technician makes an adjustment to the missile's guidance system. *(Novosti)*

An SA-2 ready for raising into launch position on its mobile pad. The North Vietnamese found they had to fire a high number of SAMs for every US aircraft destroyed and missiles were never effective enough to replace guns. *(Novosti)*

(tasked with tactical strikes) to operate in less hostile areas in the South. Douglas RB-66 Destroyers assisted these operations by providing an anti-radar screen for F-105s and a guidance system for detecting targets shrouded in mist or cloud. Reconnaissance had by 1965, determined that the North Vietnamese had some 2,000 AAA guns, primarily of 37 mm and 57 mm calibre with a few 85 mm and 100 mm weapons for good measure. At lower altitudes there was a veritable sea of smaller calibre weapons (right down to rifles carried by peasant workers) which could and did prove lethal to low flying jet aircraft, even one with the high performance of the Thunderchief.

On 5 April a SAC U-2 brought back ominous evidence that the enemy would not need to rely solely on artillery to protect himself — he also had supplies of Soviet-designed SA-2 Guideline surface-to-air missiles. Established on numerous sites, the SA-2 was highly mobile and, by camouflage and the building of dummy sites, the wily North Vietnamese deceived US aircrews into believing they were up against far more SAMs than there actually were. As well as SAMs, the North Vietnamese Air Force had fifty to sixty MiG-17s and a handful of Il-28 light bombers. Operating in conjunction with AAA and SAMs, they constituted part of one of the most formidable anti-aircraft defences ever devised.

By utilising the rugged F-105, USAF planners estimated correctly that they could meet strike requirements economically, the type having the performance necessary to usually get itself out of trouble. That this was true began to be reflected in torn and battered airframes in the base repair shops at Takhli and Korat. Despite the defences the 'Thuds' were generally able to hit the targets and cause them damage. However the terrain and the weather mitigated against really devastating strikes; the annual northeast monsoon, from mid-October to mid-March, brought torrential rainfall and a blanket of impenetrable ground mist to mask targets and prevent reconnaissance from post-bombing assessment of damage. The jungle-covered landscape not only provided good target cover — it hid downed crewmen from rescue flights. The latter became an integral part of air operations and many epic rescues were accomplished throughout hostilities, USAF helicopter crews often racing to get men out before they could be captured.

It was when Thunderchief flights began to be intercepted by the NVNAF that TAC had to look at the best way to protect its strike squadrons from MiGs. During early Rolling Thunder operations the small number of enemy fighters used to intercept did not cause widespread losses — but they were successful in that the heavily-laden 'Thuds' were forced to jettison their bomb loads in order to fight the nimble MiGs on more equal terms. What was needed was a fighter able to protect the strikes and, as had happened in Korea, there was only one type that could handle the situation. In 1950 it had been the F-86 Sabre. In 1965 it was the F-4 Phantom.

# Chapter 2
# Tactics of battle

Third of TAC's Fighter Wings to convert to Phantoms, the 8th received its first aircraft in 1965 and was guided through transition training on the new type by the incumbent CO, Colonel Joseph G. Wilson. He was to see the 'Wolfpack' established in Thailand and embark on its first war sorties for twelve years. Movement to SE Asia was completed by 8 December and the Wing's two 'permanent' Squadrons, the 433rd and 497th, organised themselves at Ubon.

The year the 'Wolfpack' arrived in Thailand had seen the end of the 'advisory' phase of US intervention in Vietnam and a definite trend towards American control of a gradually escalating series of combat operations. Despite this fact the movement of combat squadrons into the theatre was, at least officially, a low-key affair, not publicised to any degree. Even less was admitted about the presence in Thailand.

Configured for a MIGCAP these F-4Cs were photographed on take off from Da Nang in 1965. *(USAF)*

Major Tran Hanh (left) was a MiG-17F pilot who claimed an F-105 on 4 April 1965. Examining gun camera film with him is 3rd Company CO 1/Lt Pham Ngoc Lan. Qualified on the MiG-17F and MiG-21, he shot down an A-4 Skyhawk on 3 April 1965. *(Via C. Shores)*

In common with previous F-4 and F-105 deployments, the 8th TFW's F-4Cs employed flight refuelling en route to its new operational area; under the code name Young Tiger, SAC had organised its tanker force so that a part of it was continually on hand to support fighter bombers from 1964. Following a request from TAC for this service, the first air-to-air fuel transfer for a SE Asian tactical strike force was made on 9 June when four KC-135s from Clark AB replenished eight F-100s over the Da Nang area.

The plan was initially that TAC would deploy its own tankers to Asia but a grounding order placed on its obsolete KB-50 fleet led to the USAF deciding that SAC's KC-135s could be made available more quickly. A deadline had been set for 31 January 1965, by which time Don Muang had been recommended as a suitable tanker base 'in-theatre', with the main base remaining at Kadena, Okinawa. Young Tiger tankers, otherwise the 4252nd Strategic Wing, were activated on 12th January 1965, in time for the first deployment of F-4Cs of the 12th TFW.

Aerial refuelling became, often literally, a life-line to TAC fighter-bomber crews flying the strike missions to the North. The 4252nd positioned its KC-135s so that there would be at least one for every eight fighters, assuming that each required 8,000 (3,629 kg) lb of fuel in a single transfer. In practice the ratio became one tanker to every four fighters as the 4252nd utilised more bases and aircraft to keep

An F-4C poised below a KC-135 tanker en route to a North Vietnamese target. To help the tanker boom operator, a dayglo red panel highlighted the refuelling receptacle. *(MDC)*

pace with the ever-mounting sortie rate. Within six months of flying its first war-support mission, the unit was averaging 600 sorties a month, solely in support of TAC aircraft.

Refuelling areas were revised as the air war grew more intensive, as were the procedures followed by the tanker crews. At first there was an advisory restriction on operating any further north than the 19th parallel as it was thought that North Vietnamese AAA and SAMs could pose a threat. Fortunately, this did not materialise, although F-4s were made available to protect tankers. Refuelling of strike force aircraft took place mainly over Thailand or the Gulf of Tonkin. The airspace above southern Laos had been used prior to 1965 when targets in that country were being attacked, but in general tanker crews were free to work out their own procedures. General Moran S. Tyler, first CO of the 4252nd Wing, advised crews to follow established air traffic procedures up to the rendezvous point and thereafter meet requirements from TAC aircraft as the situation demanded. It was, for example, normal for the KC-135s to pass fuel at or above 26,000 ft (7,925 m) — but a heavily laden or damaged F-4 or F-105 could be hard put to reach that altitude. There was also a restriction on refuelling below 15,000 ft (4,572 m), but in the light of operational experience it was occasionally necessary to fly as low as 5,000 ft (1,524 m). The job was to get the TAC fighters home safely and an F-4 burned fuel at the rate of 1,000 lb (453 kg) a minute at full military power . . .

Fuel burn, or rather the results of this, was a drawback USAF Phantom crews had to cope with. Except when it helped tanker crews to spot a lost or damaged

14

aircraft, the long black twin smoke trails became a beacon in the sky to every AAA gunner in North Vietnam. McAir engineers worked on the problem and came up with a modification that made for cleaner-burning engines. This was accepted by the Navy but the real answer was some engine redesign. The USAF decided to await these, but it was estimated that it would be some considerable time before improved engines were ready.

That left combat crews to make their own efforts to reduce the J79s' smoke trails. It could be done by putting the engines in minimum burner or lower stages of burner, or cutting back one of the J79s to 'idle', all of which cut off smoke. Rapid changes of altitude could be made to confuse 'eyeball' search. But the mighty Phantom painted a very good radar picture and it was not for some time that Vietnam combat crews were given their own electronic equipment to blot out enemy radars.

Other problems manifested themselves under the rigours of combat: over a period of time in which individual aircraft were flown almost continually, early production F-4Cs revealed a tendency to leak fuel from the wing tanks. Moreover, of the 454 examples delivered during 1965-66, 85 aircraft were found also to have cracked ribs and stringers on outer wing panels. Fixes were recommended and initiated on production lines but in-theatre squadrons had at first to make repairs through cannibalisation. As the bases in Thailand became more self-sufficient and support services increased, all in-service F-4Cs allocated to the SE Asian theatre

Superb view of early pre-coded F-4Cs taking on fuel from a KC-135. Flight refuelling was vital to the success of the Rolling Thunder bombing campaign against North Vietnam. *(MDC)*

Markings transition. In the field camouflage being applied to F-4Cs. Note variation in radome colours. *(USAF)*

(and elsewhere) were modified by the Air Force. Later production F-4Cs and 'Ds had heavier outer wing panel stringers and an extra rib.

Air Force technicians were immeasurably assisted by a 225-man team of McDonnell Douglas 'tech reps' who followed the Phantoms to Thailand and Vietnam and served tours of duty that averaged between six and nine months. Some returned, like their aircrew customers, for two or more tours.

Many of the men who served the F-4's needs in SE Asia now hold senior engineering positions at McAir. Their view of those times is that it was part of their job to go into a combat zone — it was as simple as that. Joe Cowan, for example, grew to like Thailand so much that he spent more than seven years there, putting in a regular 100 to 125 hours a week. In an area where off-duty diversions were few, the civilian 'fixers' tended to stay on the bases and ensure that the company product remained on the top line. There was considerable personal pride in doing that. And at times the tech reps would be a sympathetic ear to the young pilots, especially if a mission had been particularly rough and the squadron had suffered losses. Many of them were very young and Vietnam was their first taste of combat — it hit them particularly hard when colleagues were lost in action.

Assignment to a Wing flying the F-4 in combat also brought its share of problems unconnected with the daily risk of death, injury or capture. One that the USAF had not really anticipated was fundamental to the Phantom, in that it had two seats. A two-seat front line fighter meant that the F-4 had a crew rather than one pilot, because modern weapons were, it was believed, becoming too complex for one man to handle effectively on his own. It was not that the F-4 was the first multi-seat jet type the Air Force had operated in the fighter role; there had been a number in service long before the Phantom. But aircraft such as the F-89 and F-94 were two-seaters with a more clearly-defined crew responsibility — usually pilot and radar operator. Two pilots in one aircraft was something entirely different.

Navy Phantoms, flown as they were by a pilot and RIO, represented what turned out to be a more realistic approach. Coupled with a policy that encouraged pilots and RIOs to fly together as much as possible and thereby build up a rapport, Navy Phantom crews had a noticeable advantage over their Air Force opposite numbers. By having two rated pilots in each Phantom, the Air Force followed the theory that the Aircraft Commander could pass on the benefit of his experience to his younger colleague, a kind of 'on the job' training programme, coupled with the safety aspect: should either pilot be incapacitated during a combat mission, the F-4 would not necessarily be lost if there was a second man trained to fly it.

In practice the idea proved largely unworkable. A situation developed which was partly the direct result of general inexperience on the F-4, and an Air Force

Reconnaissance quickly covered North Vietnam's SAM sites and the locations of most of them were well known to US intelligence. The Fan Song radar is marked at centre right. *(USAF)*

RADAR

BAMBOO MATTING

The North Vietnamese Air Force strength and disposition was also an open secret to aerial reconnaissance. These MiG-17s were seen on Phuc Yen, one of the most important military airfields in the North. *(USAF)*

failure to encourage the maintenance of crew integrity. At the start of the F-4's operational career in Vietnam very few pilots had — or indeed could have had in view of the aircraft's recent introduction to service - sufficient experience on the type for them to fly the aircraft to its limits, let alone pass this scant knowledge to the 'guy in back'. And there were quite a number of men who had been in the single-seat fighter business for years, by definition a highly individualistic profession. These men were often unwilling to share piloting with another. At times it was even said that older pilots refused to acknowledge the existence of the man in the back seat!

Even when there was a desire for a Phantom crew to work as a team, it often happened that over a long period the GIB flew with a different pilot on each mission, with the result that each crew had to start afresh. This system would have been hardly practical under peacetime conditions — in a war it was ludicrous. Having to in effect 'prove himself' to a new Aircraft Commander every time he flew was, to say the least, difficult for the pilot. The Phantom back-seater also had awesome responsibility. His primary task was to operate the radar, interpret correctly what his 'scope showed and pass succinct, accurate reports to his AC. In addition, a good GIB would at any given time know the fuel state of the

18

aircraft, its position, altitude and proximity to friendly forces, where the nearest tanker was orbiting, how far it was to the nearest safe area, which direction to steer for home base, and numerous other 'housekeeping' duties which could mean the difference between a successful mission and one that resulted in losses, particularly if the F-4 was on MiGCAP, protecting strike forces.

For all this work, the GIB reckoned his contribution deserved more than thanks if the aircraft managed to score an aerial kill. The Air Force thought so too — but there were many Aircraft Commanders who saw this as the last straw. Not only would the GIB merely be 'along for the ride' (as some Aircraft Commanders saw it) but would receive equal credit for the shoot-down which he and he alone (as he also saw it) had achieved.

Controversy raged. And it still is a subject for heated debate among fighter pilots.

The Phantom back-seater had further problems. Even if his training developed as his missions piled up and he could theoretically look forward to transferring to

The proliferation of AAA sites was harder to keep track of, but reconnaissance sorties covered the majority adjacent to likely targets and those covering US ingress-egress routes. These gunners were surprised by the camera aircraft. (USAF)

the front seat position, under the USAF's training policy the experienced GIB would have to volunteer for a further combat tour — whereupon he could, as the war accelerated, find himself faced with more tough missions riding behind Aircraft Commanders with far less experience in combat than he had. It was a Catch 22 situation of the worst kind.

Things eventually got so bad that the Air Force revised its own rules for F-4 crews to bring them more into line with those of the Navy. Subsequent to 1968 it was a Weapons Systems Operator or simply a 'navigator' rather than a pilot who occupied the Phantom's back seat. This improved matters to some extent although the ex-GIB who had achieved front seat status could then find himself teamed with a youngster who had completed the WSO course of only ten missions. Such was the complexity of the aircraft's systems, the air combat environment and the sheer overall workload that the back-seater found ten missions counted as nothing more than a 'toe in the water'. To 'swim' strongly it was estimated that a hundred missions were necessary.

It was said that some navigators actually flying combat missions over North Vietnam (those out of Stateside flight schools) had so little experience that they even had difficulty in interpreting and operating the radar. Non-operational practice flights over Thailand alleviated the situation to some degree; at least by introducing the Aircraft Commander/WSO crew complement, the Air Force had at last made some attempt to sort out a situation that was, to say the least, less efficient than it might have been. By trying to spread F-4 crew experience wide rather than deep, the Air Force had seriously underestimated the morale problem that resulted. Officially giving the back-seater credit for his invaluable contribution to aerial victory went a long way to overcome this, but continual crew rotation was bound to bring its share of problems.

Superlative aircraft though the Phantom turned out to be, and one of the most important acquisitions by Tactical Air Command in its entire history, it possessed certain flight characteristics that under some conditions could be highly dangerous. One was a direct result of its Naval origins. The problem revealed itself as the Vietnam air war widened and USAF crews were tasked with the full spectrum of missions inherent in a multi-role fighter which often obliged them to make violent manoeuvres at high gross weights at low altitude. In doing so an alarming number of Phantoms stalled out and crashed.

Early in the design stage of the F-4B, this characteristic had been known - but it was an allowable drawback because it was thought unlikely that Navy aircraft would enter such a flight envelope, or at least not very often. Certainly it was not imagined that the F-4B would seek combat at high gross weights. By keeping the 'fleet defence' external load to a minimum — a selection of Sparrow and/or Sidewinder AAMs plus fuel tanks(which would in any event be jettisoned before combat was joined), there would be no weight penalty. This was one reason why the unique semi-recessed Sparrow missile arrangement was chosen.

During carrier approaches, tests with early production aircraft proved that the F-4B would be even lighter, having burned off its internal fuel load. The type was invariably landed-on at well within its stalling angle of attack; when it was known that hauling back on the stick at low airspeeds could induce the stall and spin, pilots were trained to avoid doing so. This advice was passed onto the USAF which also, initially at least, accepted the problem. However, when F-4C crews

Vital to the war effort were EC-121 Constellations initially code named Big Eye, later College Eye or Disco. Orbiting high above the battlefield they gave strike forces timely warning of MiG activity. *(MAP)*

entered an arena such as that over North Vietnam, the hard manoeuvre out of a dangerous situation (be it from enemy fighters, AAA fire or SAMs) became the rule rather than the exception. Phantom losses began to mount.

Overcoming the stalling (or 'departure') problem had for the time being to be a matter of piloting skill in 1965. Later some wing redesign would significantly improve the Phantom's flying characteristics; in the meantime combat crews had to exercise caution and try to avoid dogfighting at low altitude.

The enormous power-to-weight ratio of the F-4C was a fundamental reason why it became such a good combat aircraft — but while capable hands made it almost 'idiot proof', the hands on the controls had to know its limits. Fortunately the Phantom Wings in Thailand had a nucleus of highly qualified command pilots whose long service and full log books (sometimes dating back to World War 2) enabled them to handle the requirements of 1960s' combat flying in an aircraft radically different to anything that had previously seen service.

Coupled with some operational problems with the aircraft they flew, these men also had to come to terms with some of the most restrictive flying parameters any combat pilot anywhere had ever had to face. A great many of them thought that very little about the Vietnam war made any sense — but to their credit they carried out the job and the United States was fortunate in having individuals who were not only well motivated to the job (however crazy it seemed to be) but had the initiative to plan ways to put their skills to the test in traditional fighter pilot fashion. So it was that a Ubon-based F-4C notched up the first kill of the war for a USAF Phantom on 10 July 1965 by employing tactics that fooled the NVNAF into taking on what they believed was a lesser adversary. The victory went to aircraft of the 45th TFS.

In this first encounter in which the MiG pilots lost the initiative because they thought they were engaging F-105s, the F-4 pilots flew at altitudes and airspeeds which suggested to the enemy radar operators that they were indeed Thunderchiefs. It had been noted by pilots of the 45th and other squadrons that the MiGs based at Phuc Yen timed their attacks on US formations when the escort was critically low on fuel and forced to make directly for home. This tactic was confirmed by Big Eye airborne early warning aircraft which passed details of MiG activity to the US strike forces. First came a yellow 'MiGs airborne' warning, followed by a red 'MiGs approaching' signal. The latter indicated that enemy aircraft were within ten minutes' flight time of the attackers. Invariably the next warning would be condition yellow as the MiGs waited. As the last flight egressed the area having carried out its attack, the red warning would be given again, and this time interception could be expected.

On 10 July the 45th TFS's flight of four F-4Cs delayed take-off for twenty minutes, timing its arrival in the combat area at fifteen minutes later than usual. Target for the day was the Yen Bai ordnance and ammunition depot and, after refuelling, the quartet of F-4s headed north at Mach.85, maintaining an altitude of 20,000 ft (6,096 m) — giving a radar plot very similar to that of an F-105 flight.

Adopting a 'fluid four' formation which gave F-4 crews good visibility and mutual cover with each element of two separated by about 5,000 ft (1,524 m), the Phantoms entered enemy airspace. Each aircraft was armed with four AIM-7 Sparrow and four AIM-9 Sidewinder AAMs; both weapons and formation became the standard for future MiG engagements in the theatre, the 45th helping to 'write the book' during its short stay in Thailand. The squadron was only on combat operations from April to August and did not thereafter return to SE Asia. In that time squadron F-4C crews downed the first two MiGs to fall in the conflict.

Having arrived in the target area the four F-4C crews maintained radar and eyeball search. Keeping radio silence to stretch the secret as long as possible, the two flights became separated, flight leader Major Richard Hall with First Lieutenant George Larson and Captains Harold Anderson and Wilbur Anderson in aircraft number two picking up MiG contacts while spreading out to gain the desired seven to eight miles (11-13 km) distance between flights. This spacing was necessary in order to avoid any missile homing on friendly aircraft that were too near, and to give the AAMs a clear target — modern air combat needs plenty of sky.

Flying aircraft numbers three and four were Captains Kenneth Holcombe and Arthur Clark and Captains Thomas Roberts and Ronald Anderson respectively. It was Holcombe and Roberts who scored. Breaking into the MiG-17s, the Phantoms avoided enemy cannon fire and used their speed to break away. Although they were able to turn more tightly, the MiGs could be overhauled with ease by the F-4, particularly when using engine afterburner.

After a misunderstanding of his back-seater's call that the radar was out, Holcombe selected boresight mode (visual weapons aiming) instead of heat (radar lock-on and fire). Firing two AIM-9Bs Holcombe saw one of them explode near the MiG in front of him. Launching two more Sidewinders, Holcombe was not immediately aware of the result, but the fireball he saw entering cloud was confirmed as his kill.

Roberts also fired all his Sidewinders at a MiG-17, the third of which did the damage. It went down inverted as the F-4s received a flak warning. Roberts was down to 6,000 ft (1,829 m) by then, and it was time to leave.

# Chapter 3
# Give and take

The sporadic nature of air combat over North Vietnam was to last almost as long as the US involvement; there were few periods when large numbers of MiGs were seen in the sky on a regular basis, as there were for example in Korea. However, the very lack of sizeable formations of enemy fighters produced difficult, if not insuperable problems. To counter fast 'hit and run' attacks on strike forces, F-4 MiGCAP patrols were essential. The presence of Phantoms became fundamental to the success of bombing missions, just as fighter escort had proved to be vital to US daylight bombing in World War 2. Re-inventing the wheel this may have been but there was no doubt that in many respects, despite the sophistication of weaponry deployed in Vietnam, the basic aims of air operations had changed little.

It should perhaps be emphasised that officially, shooting down MiGs had a very low priority. Only when they offered a direct threat to a strike were they to be engaged. The USAF recognised that blunting the enemy's air intercept capability was a bonus but the prime object of Rolling Thunder was to place enough bombs on the targets to demonstrate to the North Vietnamese the folly of continued aggression against a government friendly to the US. Red-blooded fighter pilots did not always see it that way. They were in the front line and their job, which their country had spent thousands of dollars training them to do, was to fight the other man in the air. MiG-killing represented a personal achievement, proof that they had the ability to beat the best the enemy could put up. It was not that they were bent on flouting the rules, dubious as these were. But in a gut-wrenching, sweat-soaked dogfight they held the cards. And the MiG that fell today would not be a threat tomorrow . . .

For the 8th TFW the first two of a string of MiG victories were scored on 23 April 1966 when F-4Cs of the famed 'Triple Nickel' Squadron, the 555th TFS, downed a pair of MiG-17s. Combat was opened when a flight of four F-4Cs detected four MiGs while screening Thunderchiefs attacking the Bac Giang highway and railway bridges, 25 miles (40 km) north-east of Hanoi.

Picked up on radar while they were still about fifteen miles (24 km) away, the F-4s met the MiGs in a near head-on pass. Flying the number three position were Captain Max Cameron and First Lieutenant Robert E. Evans, with Captain Robert Blake and First Lieutenant S. George in number four. Both crews observed the flight leader and the number two F-4C try difficult shots with one Sparrow each.

Cameron tried a Sidewinder. All three US missiles went wide. There ensued a ten-minute left-turning engagement between 10,000 and 18,000 ft (3,050-5,490 m) during which three MiGs set up firing passes on the number two F-4, one firing his cannon without achieving hits.

Cameron and Evans selected this trio of MiGs and quickly loosed an AIM-9 at the leader. Hardly had they had time to observe the results before the Phantom crew latched onto the second MiG which was then behind the flight leader's wingman. From his rear seat, Evans saw the MiG which his front-seater Cameron had fired at go down, falling apart and trailing thick smoke. It was felt that the Sidewinder had homed on to the MiG's tailpipe.

A second MiG had meanwhile manoeuvred into a firing position on the aircraft flown respectively by Cameron and Blake, but was unable to follow as they executed a climb and roll down to the right, coming in behind him. The enemy pilot went into a power dive towards a valley. Blake followed, firing a Sparrow. This missile was released at a bad angle so, aligning himself better, the American fired another. This time his aim was true and the MiG went in, streaming smoke.

MiG activity was apparent again on 26 April, and on the 29th Major Paul Gilmore and First Lieutenant William Smith of the 35th TFW scored a memorable kill — the first NVNAF MiG-21 confirmed in the Vietnam war. Gilmore and Smith were leading two other F-4s covering a pair of RB-66s on a reconnaissance sortie. Heading for the Red River, the formation split, one F-4 and one RB-66 proceeding on a separate mission. Gilmore and the other Phantom escorted the remaining RB-66 north-east of Hanoi. Almost immediately three MiGs were seen closing rapidly from the two o'clock position. The RB-66 departed the area as the Phantom crews dropped their external tanks and hit their afterburners, making hard left diving turns. Pulling up out of a vertical reversal at 12,000 ft (3,658 m), Gilmore and his wingman went after the MiGs which were then heading north-west in afterburner at 30,000 ft (9,144 m).

With one MiG descending very slowly trailing white vapour, the F-4s pursued the first aircraft which was making gentle clearing turns as it climbed away. Out of range for a Sparrow lock-on, Gilmore closed to 3,000 ft (914 m) and fired a Sidewinder, quickly breaking left. As a result he did not see the missile impact and kept on after his quarry. This action surprised Gilmore's wingman, who had seen the enemy pilot eject, but who could not call in as his radio was giving trouble. Gilmore pressed on with the kill, not realising there was no longer a pilot at the controls. A second Sidewinder had no effect and Gilmore fired a third with good lock-on again from 3,000 ft.

'Disgusted' at his performance, Gilmore was more satisfied when the third AIM-9 blew off the MiG's tail. Both F-4 crews watched the debris fall, then pulled up. Another MiG-21 was onto his wingman and Gilmore called a break. Coming out of the roll Gilmore saw the MiG ahead and went into afterburner, climbing. Directly behind the enemy aircraft he fired his fourth and last Sidewinder — at too short a range. The missile passed harmlessly over the MiG's left wing. Both F-4s were then low on fuel after six minutes' aerial duelling, and were forced to break off. It had been Paul Gilmore's first encounter with an enemy aircraft after, as he later put it, 'twelve years in the tactical fighter business'.

This action and others highlighted a problem faced by USAF Phantom crews early in the war — the unreliability of AAMs at close ranges. Pilots pressing home their attacks close in found that the only weapons they had could streak harmlessly past their prey. At such times formation keeping and good visual scanning were vital if they themselves were not to be damaged or shot down by their own rogue Sidewinders or Sparrows. What USAF pilots really needed when fighting got almost 'hand to hand', was a gun.

Total reliance upon missile armament was a result of the 1950's thinking that interceptors would have as their targets high-flying bombers against which only AAMs would have been effective. Despite the air combat successes of the Korean War, during the Cold War years the gun had tended to be regarded as an obsolete and outmoded weapon for fighters. It is remarkable therefore that very few US first line fighters were actually limited to all-missile armament and that the F-4 was the one aircraft which found the lack of a gun a drawback in actual combat. Fortunately for the USAF, the situation was rectified, firstly by use of detachable gun pods and later by installation of a 20 mm gun in the F-4E. For the US Navy and Marine Corps F-4 squadrons flying combat over Vietnam, though, the AAM was to remain their sole air combat weapon.

As things transpired, air-to-air missiles were nevertheless responsible for the majority of kills scored by USAF Phantom crews over Vietnam, proving if nothing else that the 'learning curve' had had significant results. The war was, after all, the first time that opposing forces were flying very high performance jet aircraft; it took time to understand the limitations of each other's machines and to work out the best tactics for dealing with them. The F-4s' crews' minor drawback in occasionally finding themselves unarmed having expended all missiles would not have been such a problem had the North Vietnamese not been flying the outdated MiG-17 and MiG-19 complete with old-fashioned (but effective) cannon armament. When the MiG-21 made its appearance, the Americans were up against a potentially more deadly opponent armed with both guns and occasionally, missiles.

Having a gun built-in from the start gave the F-105 Thunderchief a slight but significant advantage when attacked by more nimble and manoeuvrable adversaries. 'Thud' pilots used their single cannon to good effect, the first of 27 MiG-17s being shot down on 29 June 1966.

There were other occasions when sheer piloting skill gave the Americans the edge. On 29 April 1966 the 8th Wing was back in action, the first MiG downed by 'manoeuvring' being claimed by Captain Larry Keith and First Lieutenant Robert Bleakey of the 555th TFS. Flying MiGCAP for F-105s attacking the Bac Giang bridge about 25 miles (40 km) north-east of Hanoi, the F-4s found four MiG-17s to the north of the strike area. Keith was flight leader.

One MiG fell to the F-4C flown by Captain William Dowell and First Lieutenant Halbert Gossard, who despatched the enemy fighter with an AIM-9. Observing this combat, Keith broke away in the opposite direction. He saw one MiG lining up on Gossard and fired one of his own Sidewinders to distract the pilot. As the MiG took evasive action, Keith took off after him and closed to 6,000 ft (1,830 m). Starting to get a good Sidewinder tone prior to the missile locking on to its target, Keith saw the NVNAF pilot roll inverted to the left at a height of 2,500 ft (760 m). He did not recover and the MiG crashed.

Recounting the combat, Keith was of the opinion that the MiG pilot either lost control or attempted a Split-S manoeuvre without enough height. It was not the last time that USAF pilots would score a kill without firing a shot.

Another MiG-17 was to fall to an F-4C of the Triple Nickel squadron on 30 April, Captain Lawrence Golberg and First Lieutenant Gerald Hardgrave being the victors. Four Phantoms were flying a RESCAP over two pilots down about 100 miles (160 km) west-north-west of Hanoi, the two elements of two aircraft alternating with each other while air refuelling took place. Suddenly four MiG-17s attacked out of the sun. Apparently under ground control, the enemy fighters were headed directly for the F-4s when aircraft number three sighted them, about five miles (8 km) away. Manoeuvring into a favourable position Golberg and Hardgrave fired a Sidewinder which guided onto the tailpipe of one of the MiGs, which promptly exploded. Low on fuel by that time, Golberg and his wingman headed south. They put down at Udorn with about 400 lb (180 kg) of fuel left.

There followed another period when the air combat claims fell not to the Wolfpack but to its sister F-4C squadrons attached to the 35th and 388th Wings. Not before 16 September would the 8th return another confirmed kill.

During the week of 17-23 September 1966 there were 32 encounters with NVNAF MiGs. This photo caught two MiG-17s at Phuc Yen on 4 October. *(USAF)*

# Chapter 4
# Rain of bombs

By the autumn of 1966 there was still little or no sign that Hanoi's leaders were preparing to come to the conference table, or that guerrilla activity in South Vietnam was in any way curtailed. Neither the 'out country' war against the North's sources of supply, nor the high rate of sorties in the South seemed to have blunted the offensive. While air strikes killed many enemy combatants, the American failure to commit enough troops to fight a conventional ground-gaining war with established front lines meant that it fell to airpower to be the key to winning. Despite the fact that airpower alone had never before been decisive in a major war, Secretary Robert McNamara and the Joint Chiefs continued to hope it could be just that — but only under their own self-imposed rules of engagement.

With the 497th FS having been assigned to the 8th TFW on 8 December 1965 after an eighteen-month attachment which ended in December 1965, and the 555th TFS being assigned in March 1966, the Ubon Phantom wing was well up to strength to meet a renewed round of engagements with NVA MiGs. The Triple Nickel squadron had been part of the 8th Wing for a month in February/March that year and its rapidly building experience was to bring the Wolfpack results before the 555th moved away again on 1 June 1968.

All the time their airfields and support installations remained immune to US bombs, the North Vietnamese Air Force constituted a threat to US air strikes. The threat was hard to quantify due to the elusiveness of the enemy but September 1966 saw more combat recorded in which the Phantoms again demonstrated their superiority.

During his tenure as Commander of the Wolfpack, Colonel Robin Olds did what he could to initiate practical moves to streamline the operations of his unit, and to boost morale. One was, in the spring of 1967, to assign specific F-4s to individual Aircraft Commanders — because as well as the widespread rotation of crews within squadrons, men scheduled to fly missions on any given day tended to fly the aircraft that the maintenance crews provided, and it was rare for them to fly the same machine on successive missions. Apart from the obvious need to overhaul and repair aircraft damaged in combat or in the shops for routine maintenance, Olds' move enabled a degree of 'personalisation' of individual F-4s, thus carrying on a tradition that had proved to be so popular in World War 2 and Korea. The practice of applying names and cartoons, unit awards, and most of all, MiG kills, consequently flourished, if only until higher authority made moves to

F-4Cs echeloned out from an EB-66 pathfinder on a mission over the North in January 1966. The effectiveness of camouflage is well demonstrated by two of the Phantoms. *(USAF)*

discourage it. An impending 'brass visit' would occasionally see the individual markings covered by a quick coat of paint, only to re-appear again at a later date. Olds himself perpetuated the tradition of naming the aircraft he had flown in World War 2 to his F-4s, adding the appropriate suffix numbers. His most famous F-4C was probably 'Scat XXVII', although there were others flown by him and appropriately marked.

Unit badges were also carried at different periods and the 8th TFW was widely acknowledged to have applied some of the most colourful markings in the theatre, and each of the squadrons assigned to the Wing had their own traditions and nicknames — 'Satan's Angels' (433rd TFS); 'Eagle Squadron' (435th TFS) and 'Night Owls' (497th TFS). On rotation later would come the 'Assam Dragons' (25th TFS) replacing the 555th TFS, 'Triple Nickel'. But the 555th was very much part of the Wolfpack on 16 September 1966. The squadron was conducting a strike on the Dap Cau highway/railway bridge over the Canal De Rapides on the north-east rail link into Hanoi from China. At least four MiG-17s were seen by a flight of three F-4s of the 555th, operating in a combined strike/MiGCAP role. In the ensuing air battle, the element leader fired all four of his Sidewinders and two Sparrows, without scoring on any of the several MiGs he aimed at. The second Phantom (number three in the flight) was lost after manoeuvring with two of the enemy fighters and the only kill of the day went to First Lieutenants Jerry Jameson and Douglas Rose. Still carrying their ordnance as they went into the dogfight, the F-4s were at a definite disadvantage. Jameson thought the situation 'unreal'. 'For three to four minutes,' he later told newsman, 'I didn't realise what I was doing. I was just hanging on, trying to get away from a MiG that was chasing me. After I got away, I started putting into practice what I had learned in training.'

Settling down, Jameson attempted to get behind one of the MiGs but the more manoeuvrable enemy aircraft promptly executed a tight turn and latched onto the F-4's tail. As the MiG pilot fired his cannon, Jameson went to afterburner and threw the F-4 into a hard left turn followed quickly by a hard right turn to shake off his adversary. This he succeeded in doing and at that point, jettisoned his ordnance and external tanks. Back in the fray at considerably lighter weight,

On a signal from the EB-66 F-4 and F-105 formations delivered their bombs on numerous occasions when targets were obscured by clouds. (USAF)

Robin Olds conducts his pre-flight check on a 433rd TFS Phantom which boldly displays the unit insignia. One of the foremost exponents of the F-4 in Vietnam, Olds just missed becoming an ace. *(USAF)*

Jameson spotted a MiG dead ahead but was unable to pick it up on radar and could not launch a Sparrow. He overshot, ignited the burner and made another hard right turn. There was another MiG at twelve o'clock.

'At about a mile out I fired two missiles. Then I turned hard to the left and back to the right again to get away from another MiG that had begun firing on me. When I straightened out I saw debris and a man in the air'.

One thing that had attracted the USAF to the F-4 was its extremely strong structure and inherent load-carrying capability. Able to lift over 10,000 lb (4,536 kg) in a very wide combination of free fall 'iron bombs', napalm, cluster bombs and rocket packs, the F-4Cs assigned to the SE Asian theatre began to be used in strike roles as well as 'pure' escort fighters. Attrition rate of the F-105 force rose alarmingly in the first two years of Rolling Thunder and it was with some relief that TAC was able to deploy the Phantom — which was, unlike the F-105, currently in production. Various projections were made, assuming that the war went on at the current pace of operations, as to when the F-105 would become totally extinct . . .

The campaign against North Vietnam was periodically interrupted by 'bombing pauses' initiated by Lyndon Johnson to give the enemy a chance to negotiate a peace settlement. The North Vietnamese instead used the freedom from US air strikes to repair shattered rail and road links with their communist neighbours and to further strengthen their defences. The US in its turn, looked to its own equipment and methods employed in the air war; numerous changes were made during the mid-1960s and implemented for future deployment, as a result of which, by the end of the decade the USAF was a far more efficient and technically well-equipped force than it had been at the start of operations against the North. The multi-role Phantom was developed to undertake new tasks, some of which had hardly been known about, let alone budgeted for or developed into hardware, when it entered service.

The early production F-4C had for example, few aids to accurate bomb aiming and many USAF sorties were led to their targets by EB-66s equipped as 'pathfinders'. On a pre-arranged signal the pathfinder aircraft would order weapons release, the F-4 pilots 'pattern' bombing from altitudes above the flak.

While it was primarily a Phantom Wing in the decade or so it undertook South-East Asian combat operations, the 8th TFW operated two gunship adaptations of

A well-weathered F-4C keeping a good look out for the opposition over North Vietnam. *(USAF)*

Destined not to see extensive service in Vietnam was the F-104C Starfighter. It was however, combat tested twice at different periods. This example, *56-904*, shows the original natural aluminium finish of aircraft making the first deployment with the 479th TFW. *(Lockheed)*

transports, the AC-123 and AC-130, as well as the B-57 and the F-104 Starfighter for brief periods. The Canberra and gunships entered service after the cessation of Rolling Thunder, but the F-104 was one of a long list of types that the USAF combat tested in the mid-1960s. While Vietnam was not the sort of war that some of these aircraft had been designed for — indeed, it was far more arduous on aircraft systems than for example, a European battleground might have been — it showed up the kind of requirements demanded of first line combat aircraft in 'current' wars.

The F-104 was representative of a type designed in the 1950s for a role totally different to the conditions prevailing in Vietnam — in fact so many of the West's fighters were intended for the interception of high flying bombers, that ground attack took something of a back seat. This legacy of a decade with its Cold War overtones of a massed bomber strike against the continental USA, spawned a whole range of interceptors which were never called upon to undertake that task. And when the predominantly tactical war in Vietnam came about, the USAF tried to find alternative employment for aircraft such as the Starfighter, with varying degrees of success.

The F-104 version used in Vietnam was the C model with the J-79-GE-7A engine offering 1,000 lb (453 kg) more thrust than that of the F-104B, an updated fire control system which could operate by day or night, and a probe-and-drogue aerial refuelling system. The aircraft were deployed to SE Asia in 1965, Tactical Air Command having accepted 77 examples to equip the 479th Tactical Fighter Wing, beginning mid-October 1958.

The Wing's aircraft were based at Da Nang and flew air defence, escort and ground attack sorties from 20 April 1965, when the first fifteen aircraft arrived, to 20 November that year. At the completion of their temporary duty, F-104s had

Back in South East Asia in 1966 the 435th TFS flew another tour of duty under the command of the Wolfpack. This photograph shows F-104C-5 *56-890* being serviced under floodlighting at Ubon during the cool night hours. *(Lockheed)*

flown 2,937 sorties. They then returned to the US, having suffered some losses, mainly to ground fire. A year later, the Starfighter was back, based this time at Udorn, Thailand, where the 479th Wing's 435th Squadron was placed under the operational jurisdiction of the 8th TFW. Having gone through the Project Grindstone modification programme, these F-104Cs were better suited to Vietnam combat by being able to carry up to four AIM-9B Sidewinders (the normal fit being two) and a range of ordnance, including various bombs and 2.75-inch (70 mm) FFAR packs. While it had the advantage of a built-in M-61 gun, the F-104's usefulness was limited; it could only carry 960 lb (435 kg) of ordnance and its range, without refuelling, was only 850 miles (1,368 km). With adequate numbers of F-105s with their high load carrying capability available, and a gradually building force of F-4s for escort, there was relatively little employment for another type on strike missions into the North.

It was also found that there was little need for the USAF to deploy defensive fighters to protect bases from air attack and neither the F-104 nor the F-102 (which would have shared such duty) were required on any long-term basis. The 435th TFS did, however, complete its tour of duty and returned home in July 1967. There is no record of F-104s making contact with enemy fighters despite their being flown on a number of MiG 'screen' missions to protect USAF and South Vietnamese aircraft, although the 435th did fly on some of the more well-known missions, including Operation Bolo. Four flights of F-104Cs (sixteen aircraft) acted in support of the F-4 mainforce, as did the EB-66, RC-121 and KC-135.

The apparent resilience of the North Vietnamese not only to withstand the bombing but to make good repairs in a remarkably short time, led to a shortage of munitions during 1966. Widely denied officially, it was true that air strikes were sent off with reduced loads mixed with ballast. Working under a strange logic, theatre commanders sent not a few aircraft out carrying full loads, but many hung with half or a quarter the normal quota. One F-4 pilot was interviewed about the bomb shortage after he had just landed at Da Nang. He gave vent to his feelings: 'We risked eight guys', he told a reporter, 'when we could have hung the whole load on one plane — risking only two people — and done the job better'.

Asked why he thought this action had been taken, the pilot replied: 'Damned if I know, unless it's just to keep our sortie rate high. But I'll tell you this: It's a goddamn crime.'

The pilot was not far wrong; the Vietnam war reflected an almost unbelievable US obsession with statistics. On the ground there was the notorious 'body count' of enemy casualties — in the air it was 'sortie rate', Navy versus Air Force, each service vying with the other to prove it could fly the most.

There is no doubt also that the sortie rate brought a great deal of wastage. The bombing caused widespread dispersal of supplies and — even with sophisticated reconnaissance — it was hard to be sure if an innocent looking group of huts in fact hid a petrol dump, transport or supplies throughout a country which had by necessity become an armed camp. That is why Phat Diem, a small rural hamlet of 5,500 people in the Red River delta, had been subjected to sixty air attacks by 1967 . . . It apparently had no military significance whatsoever. And there were a great many Phat Diems.

Between February 1965 and October 1968 the US was to expend one million tons of bombs and rockets against targets in North Vietnam, cratering some areas to resemble the surface of the moon. Whole map references simply disappeared under huge holes that rapidly filled with water. These craters testified to the fact that the weapons and techniques the US was using in the 1960s had not really progressed very far. Many of the targets were tiny and extremely difficult to hit, let alone destroy. Worst of all were North Vietnam's bridges. Just as in World War 2 and Korea where bridges were the target for many thousands of tons of bombs before they became impassable, so the US tried to cut off enemy supplies in the face of defences that restricted the required close-in, precision release of free fall munitions. A big industrial effort was required to develop new weapons if the air strikes on the North were to achieve lasting results.

# Chapter 5
# Masquerade

One of the most famous incidents to come out of the air war over Vietnam was Operation Bolo, the skilfully planned and executed trick played on the enemy MiG force by the 8th TFW. Devised and carried out by the Wing's pilots, it resulted in an outstandingly successful aerial engagement for the American crews who were growing increasingly frustrated at the North Vietnamese tendency to avoid air combat. Under the prevailing rules, however, there was little they could do to force the issue if their opposite numbers chose to fight only when they held a tactical advantage.

It became fairly obvious that enemy pilots were fully aware of the capability of the F-4 against their own MiGs and had probably been ordered to avoid tangling with an aircraft which, if not so agile as their smaller, lighter machines, was far more powerful, well armed with missiles to knock them down at long ranges and very much faster. For their cannon to be effective against the tough structure of Western strike aircraft and fighters, the NVNAF pilots had to close to a few thousand yards. Then they were up against crews who well knew their business — and they might have also guessed that their tactics to date had antagonised their opponents to a significant degree. Baiting a tiger was a very risky occupation.

The North Vietnamese also had little way of knowing how long the Americans would leave their airfields alone. They too flew under a most unreal set of rules.

Few men were more aware of this fact than Colonel Robin Olds, who arrived at Ubon to take command of the 8th Wing on 30 September 1966. What the veteran combat pilot found was probably without parallel in his Air Force career: here were crews more than able to handle an aircraft widely recognised as the best in the world in its class, flying sorties against a country that should, on balance, have had few opportunities to challenge them seriously. Yet the record spoke for itself. The Phantom pilots were being challenged. And they were losing aircraft, not only to ground defences but to enemy fighters. Missing from the scenario was that old reliable American superiority in tactics which had won the day in World War 2 and Korea.

Numbers were not making much difference; although the Americans had long enjoyed a generous supply of superb equipment and enviable training, neither it seemed were being used to anywhere near full advantage. Olds and others knew full well the real reason for this but for the time being his men had to make the best of the situation.

Fortunately for morale, by the time Olds reached Ubon, he had something of an answer. On 22 September he had stopped over at 7th Air Force headquarters to discuss details of a plan originally devised by Captain John B. Stone, a junior officer in his new command. Olds quickly saw the merits of the plan, the crux of which was to draw the enemy into battle by posing as less-potent Thunderchiefs. It had been done successfully before but there seemed every opportunity to score a much more decisive victory. Stone's plan was enthusiastically taken up by 7th AF Commander General William W. Momyer. Olds would lead the operation as soon as practicable.

Colonel Joseph Wilson handed the reins of the wing to Robin Olds on 30 September, having served in his command capacity slightly less than the average twelve months which became the tour of duty for men who succeeded him. Colonel Olds' new command enjoyed the advantage of having pilots with much

Col Daniel "Chappie" James, Jr was vice commander of the 8th TFW during Robin Olds' tenure as CO. He later rose to four-star general rank and became commander of NORAD. *(USAF)*

experience in fighters; along with himself, Colonel Daniel 'Chappie' James had begun practising the art back in World War 2. Captain Everett T. Raspberry, Jr, and Major Philip Combies were younger men, as were John Stone, Lawrence Glynn, Jr, and Major Thomas Hirsch. All these Phantom exponents were to take advantage of the situation created by Operation Bolo.

Pre-mission planning was undoubtedly given impetus by the fact that on 2 December 1966 US air forces had suffered badly at the hands of the North Vietnamese defences — eight aircraft had been lost, all to SAMs. But if the missiles and guns were difficult to counter effectively at that period of the war, some payment could be exacted from the MiG force.

The Americans estimated, on the basis of the NVNAF's most recent showing, that the loss of five or more machines could have a significant effect. Olds and his people gambled on the proven tactics of the MiG pilots in singling out only fighter-bombers for attack. Olds would send them 'fighter bombers' — at least as far as the ground control interception radar operators were concerned. He would present a target that the enemy should be unable to resist.

To assemble his sufficiently large 'strike force' Olds drew on elements of his own wing and the 366th with Phantoms, plus the F-105-equipped 355th and 388th. While the 8th's F-4Cs would be primarily tasked with bringing the MiGs up, other elements would orbit areas where MiGs had been encountered before. The Wolfpack would be West Force with the F-4Cs of the 366th TFW making up East Force and taking on the job of covering Kep and Cat Ni airfields and blocking approach routes to and from the North.

In total the Bolo task force consisted of fourteen flights of F-4Cs (56 aircraft); six flights of F-105 Iron Hand SAM suppressors (24) and four flights of F-104s (16), supported by flights of EB-66, RC-121 and KC-135 aircraft. This sizeable force had therefore nearly 100 aircraft to combat MiGs, blind their GCI radar and hopefully, restrict the fixed ground defences and SAMs. To this end the F-4s carried for the first time QRC-160 ECM pods on outboard wing pylons, balanced on the opposite side by a fuel tank. AIM-9B Sidewinder AAMs occupied the inner wing pylons and the full complement of Sparrows was also carried.

Weather forecasts, which had in recent months offered only 'lousy' conditions, predicted that the chosen date for the operation, 2 January 1967, would be favourable. Briefings were detailed, and began as early as 30 December. Olds notified his crews that there would be a 24-hour stand-down prior to D-Day. Car company names had been used as callsigns for some months. No changes needed to be made. Crews were warned not to attempt to out-turn the MiGs or even turn with them if this could possibly be avoided. Succeeding flights had to watch out for friendly fighters, but the flights over the target areas were given unrestricted use of AAMs since all other aircraft encountered could be considered as hostile.

As take-off time approached on the 2nd, the weather deteriorated. Considerable overcast and cloud could be expected in the vicinity of the MiG bases, and a one-hour delay was called. Everything went into high gear for a 12:25 launch and Olds, Ford and Rambler flights left on schedule, followed at 12:55 by Vespa, Plymouth, Lincoln and Tempest flights. All other US aircraft were grounded to give the MiGs the chance to concentrate on Operation Bolo.

Take off was at five-minute intervals and all aircraft flew to their rendezvous points to carry out air refuelling. Tempest leader then experienced trouble in fuel transfer and aborted, in company with Tempest 02. Later the rest of Tempest flight returned home, the pilots having found their ECM pods to be inoperative.

To make the incoming mission authentic for the 'scope' watchers up north, the F-4 MiG killing force masqueraded as F-105s right down to call signs, flight profiles and communications, the latter including en route requests for Doppler checks, whereas the F-4s were equipped with INS. Approaching the target area, Colonel Olds told his pilots to 'green up' — Thud drivers' jargon for arming bombs.

With his flight 'in the green' at a point twenty miles (32 km) from Hanoi, Olds' F-4Cs headed down one of the flight corridors used by F-105s. The weather was not good — this was the one factor which could cause failure of the mission: would the North Vietnamese expect a strike in such conditions? Olds had expected reaction earlier, over the Red River or near Phuc Yen airfield, but nothing happened.

The second flight penetrated the Phuc Yen battle area at 15:05, led by Chappie James. As briefed, his Ford flight was five minutes behind Olds' aircraft. Still nothing.

Slow enemy reaction forced Olds to cancel the 'fire free' option to reduce accidental firing at friendlies who might now emerge suddenly from cloud. West Force could hardly watch airfields in such conditions and East Force had even greater difficulty in penetrating the murk. None of the 366th's pilots sighted MiGs and the cloud prevented them from entering their assigned battle area. Then Olds' flight picked up a low, very fast radar return seventeen miles (27 km) from their twelve o'clock position. The CO sent his number three to check it out. Reaching the top of the cloud layer, this crew failed to make contact as the bogey passed below the American flight. Olds and his back-seater, First Lieutenant Charles Clifton, meanwhile climbed to 12,000 ft (3,658 m) and headed towards Thud Ridge, the chain of hills northwest of Hanoi.

Resuming leadership of his flight, Olds heard James' flight report MiGs closing on Olds' flight at six o'clock. A high speed combat ensued as the MiG-21 pilots seemed aggressive.

Flying Olds' O2 on the Bolo mission were Lieutenants Ralph Wetterhahn and Jerry Sharp. Their combat report described what happened next: 'Olds 03 observed a MiG-21 at six o'clock. Olds 01 saw one at eight o'clock and Olds 02 saw one at ten o'clock. Olds 01, 02, and 03 swung left and slid between the second and third MiGs. Olds 01 fired two AIM-7Es which failed to guide, while the number three MiG began sliding to six o'clock on the three F-4s. Olds 01 fired two Sidewinders which immediately guided on the undercast. At this time Olds 02 achieved a boresight lock-on, returned the mode switch to radar, centred the dot, and salvoed two AIM-7Es. The first was felt to launch but was not observed. The second launched and it appeared just left of the radome. It guided up to the MiG-21 (range 1½ to two nautical miles) and impacted just forward of the stabiliser.

'A red fireball appeared and the MiG-21 flew through it, continued on for an instant and then swapped ends, shedding large portions of the aft section. A small fire was observed in the aft section, emitting black smoke. The aircraft went into a flat spin and rotated slowly, similar to a falling leaf, until disappearing in the clouds . . .'

About sixty seconds later Captain Walter Radeker, III, and First Lieutenant James Murray got the second kill of the mission. They chased a MiG-21 which appeared to be intent on nailing Olds 03. Obtaining a weak AIM-9 tone, Radeker poured on the coal and improved the missile's chances. Putting the seeker head into heat he launched. Achieving good guidance the Sidewinder struck the enemy fighter forward of the tail, causing a burst of black smoke and a violent tuck-under. The Americans saw it drop away trailing smoke.

Then it was Robin Olds' own turn. MiGs began popping up out of the cloud base 'all round the clock' and one happened to have Olds in sight from the Phantom's six o'clock — more, it was assumed, by chance rather than design. Olds executed a left turn to spoil the MiG pilot's deflection and then saw another one about a mile and a half away. Ignoring the first one, Olds gave chase and launched missiles, only to see his quarry disappear into cloud. But there were other targets.

Olds slammed in full afterburner and pulled in hard to gain position on this second MiG. 'I pulled the nose up high about 45 degrees, inside his circle. He was turning around to the left so I pulled the nose up high and rolled to the right. This is known as a vector roll. I got up on top of him and half upside down, hung there, and waited for him to complete more of his turn and timed it so that as I continued to roll down behind him, I'd be about twenty degrees angle off and about 4,500 to 5,000 ft [1,370-1,525 m] behind him. That's exactly what happened. Frankly I'm not sure he ever saw me. When I got down low and behind, and he was outlined by the sun against a brilliant blue sky, I let him have two Sidewinders, one of which hit and blew his right wing off.' Checking his own fuel state, Olds acknowledged Radecker's call that he was at bingo fuel state, brought his flight together and headed home.

MiG number four fell to AC Robert Raspberry flying Ford 02 with Robert Western as pilot. Rolling in to position himself at six o'clock to a MiG-21, Raspberry had no visible indication that the enemy pilot had seen the F-4. As the MiG rolled out of a turn an AIM-9B was already on its way. It detonated in the tailpipe area and blew the MiG end over end before it went into a slow spiral towards the undercast. Ford flight then departed the combat area.

Over near Phuc Yen, John Stone and Clifton Dunnegan, Jr, in Rambler 01, Lawrence Glynn and Lawrence Cary (Rambler 02) and Philip Combies and Lee Dutton (Rambler 04) became the victors of West Force, which was involved in two separate engagements. The flight experienced a degree of radio trouble from the less than reliable UHF set fitted in the Phantom. (The poor performance of this radio was later condemned roundly by the USAF's first Vietnam ace, Steve Ritchie. He had very few kind thoughts for whoever-it-was who could authorise billions of dollar's worth of funds for weapons and other high technology, state-of-the-art items, yet not be able to give his aircraft a decent radio . . .

Radio malfunction prevented Glynn from taking over as Rambler flight leader as soon as he spotted MiGs, as per briefed procedure. Neither could he alert the rest of the flight. But other members saw them soon enough.

Philip Combies was at 16,000 ft (4,877 m) flying at 540 knots when he sighted four MiG-21s in loose formation two o'clock low at six to eight miles' (9.5-13 km) range. About two miles (3.2 km) behind these were two more. Sliding right, Combies hit the burner and his pilot got a boresight, full system lock-on on one of the MiGs. He reported later: 'I had selected radar and interlocks out, as prebriefed for an ACT [Air Combat Tactics] environment. I had no difficulty in tracking the MiG. I don't think I pulled over four Gs at any time during the whole battle. Using the Navy tactic of disregarding the steering dot, I pulled lead on the MiG using the reticule. When I felt I was where I wanted to be, I pulled the trigger, released, pulled again, and held.

'I did not observe the first Sparrow at all. However, I saw the second from launch to impact at approximately 12,000 ft [3,658 m] at the time of launch. The second Sparrow impacted in the tailpipe area followed by a large orange ball of fire and a chute sighting.'

Stone and his wingman were also attacking MiGs and a second pair attempted to gain the upper hand by first diverting the Phantom crews' attention. One made a low pass and fired his cannon, without any effect. Stone broke right and reversed left to get back to the first pair of MiGs, having in the meantime lost his wingman, who had barrel-rolled high and joined aircraft number four, thinking that this was Stone's machine.

Closing in behind the original pair of MiGs, Stone and Dunnegan set up three Sparrows for launch. Having intended to fire his missiles in salvoes of two, Stone fired two after the first one went out of sight. Only one was needed. It detonated on the MiG's wing root and the aircraft caught fire, the pilot ejecting. That made six.

Glynn and Cary had followed other MiGs which had split up. In company with aircraft number four they fired two Sparrows, the second of which hit. The MiG exploded. Flying through the debris, which caused some damage to the

Among the most important items of equipment introduced on the F-4s and F-105s tasked with North Vietnam strikes was the AN/ALQ 119 ECM pod. Actively transmitting signals, a number of these pods created an electronic 'wall' which confused enemy ground radars. (R. L. Ward)

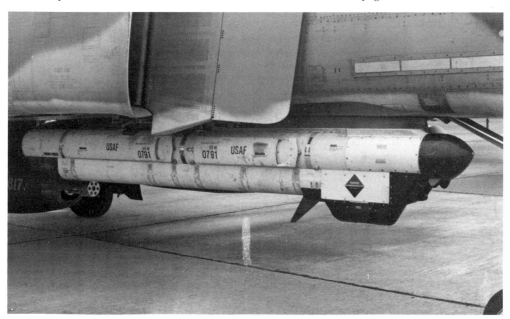

underside of his aircraft, Glynn saw the pilot bale out. He fired an AIM-7 at another enemy fighter but it passed harmlessly by.

More attacks were made by both sides. One MiG attacked Glynn with both cannon fire and eight to ten small rockets, but he broke hard left and avoided the barrage.

Seven down for no loss to the Americans was a spectacular achievement, very welcome at that stage of the war. It was estimated that the NVNAF only had about fourteen 14 MiG-21s in service before Operation Bolo. The loss was therefore the more serious to the enemy and the Phantom pilots were elated to have proved their ability to beat his best.

So successful had Operation Bolo been that it was thought unlikely that the MiGs would be caught napping a second time if a big force tried the same tactic too soon afterwards. But there was no reason why a small force might not bag a MiG by following a similar deception — so four days after Bolo the 8th TFW laid on a successful ruse sortie using just two F-4Cs masquerading as RF-4s.

Because the very nature of their work was designed to find fresh targets and assess damage already done, USAF photo reconnaissance aircraft were prime targets for North Vietnam's defences. MiGs had also attacked equally important weather recon aircraft on 3 and 4 January and forced the missions to be abandoned. On the 6th Captain Richard Pascoe and First Lieutenant Norman Wells led Major Thomas Hirsch and First Lieutenant Roger Strasswimmer off from Ubon bound for the Hanoi area.

The plan was for the Phantoms to fly close formation so that their radar picture would indicate one aircraft on a reconnaissance flight. Following one of the routes usually used by RF-4Cs, Pascoe and Hirsch encountered heavy AAA fire near Phuc Yen. Turning on his ECM pod, Pascoe saw the flak become inaccurate, missing the flight by some distance as the electronic signal blotted out the ground gunners' radar.

As the 8th had tried this trick the day before and found no action, Pascoe and Hirsch thought the MiG GCI controllers had cottoned on. The Phantoms were about 25 miles (40 km) north-west of the North Vietnamese capital before a radar contact was made. There were four MiG-21s and Pascoe wasted little time in setting up his kill. Two AIM-7s intended for the enemy flight leader launched cleanly but only one was seen to impact, on the fuselage at mid-point. The MiG burst into flames and fell in an uncontrollable dive into cloud.

Further attempts were made to knock down the rest of the MiGs in this flight, and as Pascoe engaged MiGs numbers two and three Hirsch locked onto number four. Sliding in from his five o'clock position, he fired a Sparrow with full radar computing system engaged. Going into a steep climb, the MiG appeared to slow then came down, rolling slowly. Just before it disappeared into cloud both Hirsch and Strasswimmer saw the pilot eject. Having temporarily lost sight of his missile, no detonation was seen by the F-4 crew and it was assumed that the MiG flamed out or the pilot had lost control.

# Chapter 6
# Wolfpack with guns

It was in May 1967 that the 8th TFW became the first in South East Asia to receive the new F-4D. The first 'true' Air Force version, the D model introduced a number of improvements and equipment updates. Produced as it was under 'war emergency' conditions, though, there were inevitably teething troubles. The SE Asian climate continued to play havoc with weapons release computers, the fire control system and ECM equipment. Progress had also been slow in providing the F-4 with the capability to home onto and jam enemy radars thereby creating a dedicated Wild Weasel aircraft to support and eventually replace the F-105F/G. A time-consuming and difficult task, this was compounded to a significant degree by the lack of space for much new equipment in the F-4's already packed airframe.

The first F-4D to score a MiG kill was the 555th's *66-249*. It was photographed on 5 May 1967 with appropriate red star. If the aircraft survived the war these victory markings were left on and some remain on Phantoms currently operated by Air Guard and Reserve squadrons. *(MacSorley via Pennick)*

F-4C *64-849* of the 497th TFS at Ubon in May 1967. The Wolfpack's aircraft were often marked with rudder flashes or coloured fin caps to denote the squadron, as indicated by the blue and yellow decoration of this Phantom, also marked with one MiG kill and a tiny red lion on the rudder between the two dark areas of camouflage. *(Frank MacSorley via George Pennick).*

McDonnell Douglas initiated production of the F-4D in March 1964; first flight took place on 8 December 1965 and the USAF took initial delivery that same month. Following issue of sixteen aircraft to the Fighter Weapons School at Nellis, the 33rd TFW at Eglin became the first unit to fly it. Some time passed before the F-4D was despatched to SE Asia and with the 33rd taking delivery on 21 June 1966, other F-4Ds went to Europe, so releasing more F-105s for service in Thailand. The 555th TFS was the first recipient of the new model in the 8th Wing.

Externally similar to the F-4C apart from having smooth lower nose contours where there had been an infra-red sensor on the C model, the F-4D featured improved bombing capability by having the bombing computer supply slant range radar information; also added was a stabilised lead-computing gunsight, and radar ranging and navigation systems were generally upgraded. The smooth nose configuration was shortlived, as an under-nose fairing became necessary to house Radar Homing and Warning (RHAW) aerials.

Work was also carried out to improve the Phantom's already formidable ordnance-carrying ability in the light of Vietnam combat experience, enabling it to use virtually all air-to-air and air-to-ground weapons for this class of aircraft. Not all of them turned out to be as reliable as had been hoped.

Hughes had made a good case for the AIM-4D Falcon AAM as primary F-4 armament and the F-4D was the first model equipped to use it. One of a long series of Hughes production models designed for short (about six miles/10 km) range anti-fighter combat, the AIM-4D combined a powerful rocket motor and an advanced seeker head. The Falcon supplanted the trusty AIM-9 Sidewinder for a time although its relatively high cost and complex set-up time, which included the necessity to cool the infra-red seeker prior to launch, made it an unpopular weapon in combat. Robin Olds is said to have demanded reinstatement of the

Sidewinder within 24 hours after the 8th TFW had had a chance to use the Falcon in anger . . .

Other crews shared Olds' opinion and F-4Ds were subsequently wired to use both the AIM-9 and AIM-4. Fortunately, by the time dual-missile-capable F-4Ds reached operational squadrons in June 1969, the war over North Vietnam had seen the passing of the MiG engagements of previous years.

The F-4D could also carry the SUU-16A gun pod from the outset, this weapon subsequently being replaced by the SUU-23A pod which dispensed with the ram-air turbine drive and introduced an electric motor to spin the firing mechanism. The gun remained a single M-61A1 with a maximum rate of fire of 6,000 rpm, fed by a 1,200-round magazine.

New avionics introduced on the F-4D included: APQ-109 fire control radar with air-to-ground ranging capability, replacing the APQ-100 system of the F-4C; a General Electric ASQ-91 weapons release computer was housed in a redesigned rear fuselage bay and linked to an AIResearch ASG-22 servo-sight and lead-computing amplifier and gyro; an ASN-63 INS replaced ASN-48 to take care of virtually all navigation and weapons aiming/release problems and enhanced air-to-air gunnery. Electrical power was boosted by installation of 30 kVA generators and equipment cooling was also improved.

The 435th called itself the Eagle Squadron and various bird devices (two here) were applied. This F-4D, named 'Wolfpack Lead' was flown for a time by the wing CO Col Charles Pattillo, whose name appears in white on the red canopy trim. *(Via R. L. Ward)*

The weapon most appreciated by Phantom crews was the pod-mounted gun; supplies of the SUU-16A reached the war zone in May and these were quickly rigged under F-4Cs. Combat crews could now prove what they had long believed — that a gun would have been a useful item of equipment on the F-4 right from the start. And it did not take long for the gun to prove its worth. On 14 May the 366th TFW, the first to have its F-4Cs cleared to use the SUU-16A, shot down two MiGs.

It took a little practice for crews to make allowance for the slight downward angle of fire and to compensate for some degree of inaccuracy as the pod vibrated on its pylon and spread the stream of shells, but overall there was great enthusiasm and a feeling that, considering the unreliability of missiles (particularly at close ranges), the F-4 could now dogfight with the MiGs on far more even terms.

At that time, there had been more than enough evidence to show that the F-4's primary weapon, the AIM-7D Sparrow, was next to useless against targets flying at subsonic speeds or at altitudes below 8,000 ft (2,438 m). Early Sparrows also trailed a highly visible stream of rocket motor smoke which helped the F-4 crews' intended victim to tighten his turn and get lower. Lacking sufficient manoeuvrability, the AIM-7 would often be unable to follow.

Greater success was achieved with the AIM-9, which was so simple it was said to have less electronic components than the average radio. Smaller and lighter than the Sparrow, the AIM-9B with an uncooled infra-red seeker head possessed a narrow look-angle, which meant it had to be pointed directly at the target for a good lock on. If the aiming angle was off, the seeker could be distracted by sunlight, reflections from cloud or ground heat. Found to be most effective in a stern attack where it had jet exhaust to home on to, the Sidewinder emerged from Vietnam combat as the more reliable of the two AAMs mainly carried by the F-4 on MiGCAP missions.

Combat results inevitably stimulated an intensive programme of R & D to update existing weapons and provide others to deal with new threats and targets. In the meantime, the crews soldiered on with bombs and missiles which mostly had their origins long before the war and had hitherto been subject only to test firing programmes. Their use in action often found them wanting.

On 23 April the USAF was at last cleared to make use of the reconnaissance photographs that had been piling up in 7th Air Force headquarters since before the start of Rolling Thunder — those clearly showing the location, strength and operational status of the MiG airfields in North Vietnam. Pilot frustration at the immunity these airfields enjoyed was swept away in April when both the Air Force and the Navy attacked them and began working down the list, starting with the nine with runways of over 6,000 ft (1,830 m) capable of operating jet fighters. Complying with one of the most popular command decisions since the war started, US pilots looked upon the task of taking out enemy airfields as fundamental to their main job of placing bombs on the targets. It was a job they had trained for and could do well.

Kep and Hoa Lac were the 23 April targets. Pilots found MiGs in abundance as they swept in to dump their loads. Above the strike forces, a single MiG-21 attempted to intercept F-4Cs of the 366th TFW and was swiftly despatched with a Sparrow AAM. Other MiGs flew harassing sorties and did achieve some

Factory view of the SUU-16A gun pod fitted to USAF F-4s shows to advantage the ram-air turbine mechanism of the early pod.

Similar to the SUU-16A, the SUU-23A was a step forward in pod guns. It dispensed with the turbine 'drive' and housed the entire feed mechanism inside the pod. Note the distinctive intake above the barrel shield.

The well-decorated tunic of 1/Lt Nguyen Duc Soat reflects his combat prowess. He shot down six F-4s, one of which was claimed in June 1972. *(Via C. Shores)*

dissolution of the bombing as the F-4s 'cleaned up' in order to offer combat.

Nine MiGs were confirmed as destroyed on the two bases, with three more probably damaged beyond repair. On three subsequent strikes, on 28 April and 1 and 3 May, the Americans destroyed twenty more enemy aircraft — the kind of loss ratio the NVNAF could ill-afford.

Airfield strikes marked an escalation of the US offensive against the North that gave the NVNAF little choice but to pull its aircraft back to bases in China if it was not to be annihilated. A second option was to fight — but the result of taking on the Americans had been traumatically demonstrated in the past. Not that the NVNAF did not have pilots well able to challenge US air strikes — men such as Nguyen Van Bay, Nguyen Ngoc and Mai Van Cuong could be dangerous adversaries, as their opposite numbers would be at pains to confirm. Lack of enough well qualified leaders worked against the North Vietnamese in an air force that had had to undergo intensive training on modern jet combat aircraft in a very short space of time. Limited exposure to modern technology was reflected in the fact that Van Bay was said to have not even driven a car when he embarked on an accelerated pilot training course . . .

On the international basis of five enemy aircraft destroyed in aerial combat to confirm the status of 'ace', North Vietnam produced at least fifteen by the end of the war. While some of the dates of their combat claims do not tally exactly with the losses known to the US Department of Defense, there is little doubt that North Vietnamese pilots were offered a wide variety of potential targets, from jet strike aircraft to helicopters. Unlike their adversaries, NVNAF pilots did not enjoy regular rotation after a stipulated period of time, or number of missions flown. While the American system had its drawbacks, the North Vietnamese pilot would be in the front line almost without a break, simply because the pool of suitably qualified replacements was always too small.

All the leading North Vietnamese aces flew in the 1st, 2nd or 3rd Companies, all of which were equipped with the MiG-17, -19 and -21 although the MiG-19 was only met in combat towards the end of the US involvement.

Supply of the MiG-17 by China and Russia was limited to the early versions. Simple to fly, the type was highly manoeuvrable and heavily armed with cannon. It took off at 13,200 lb (5,987 kg) to meet fighters which manoeuvred against it at

Capt Pham Thang Ngan (in cockpit) and Nguyen Van Coc indulge in a little 'hangar flying'. *(Via C. Shores)*

49

Airborne 497th TFS F-4C shows typical MiGCAP armament of AIM-9B Sidewinders and AIM-7E Sparrows. Serial No 64-848. *(MacSorley via Pennick)*

F-4D of the Assam Dragons (68-772) flying with a typical mixed load comprising 750lb low drag bombs, an ECM pod, strike camera and a single Sparrow AAM. *(USAF)* Also-ADSID ✓ p.108

around 35,000 lb (15,876 kg), the weight of a laden F-105 or F-4. To be more precise, a combat weight configured F-105D hauled 35,600 lb (16,148 kg) while an F-4D was even heavier at 38,700 lb (17,554 kg) if carrying four AIM-7s, two 370-gal (1,682 litre) external tanks and one store. Even if the F-4 crew jettisoned the store and tanks the weight of the aircraft did not fall that much and the three times as heavy factor remained when US aircraft tangled with MiGs.

In the main, North Vietnamese aerial victories were scored with cannon fire, although the MiG-21 used the K-13A Atoll AAM to some effect. Versions supplied to the North included the MiG-21F, 'PF and 'PFM, as well as the Chinese-assembled F-7 derivative. The MiG-21PF was the version most widely encountered in combat by US pilots, and the total peak inventory in front line aviation companies was around ninety. Substantial numbers of all MiG fighter models, including the MiG-15, were used by the North Vietnamese for conversion training.

A maximum speed pass by small numbers of aircraft remained one of the most economical tactics employed by the NVNAF throughout the Vietnam war; if a pilot could use the few seconds of surprise available to him before being detected by radar, he could close, shoot, and be away unscathed, probably achieving the bonus of one or more F-105s or F-4s jettisoning bombs in response to the MiG warning from orbiting surveillance aircraft.

# Chapter 7
# Three days in May

The successes against the MiG interceptions in May 1967 was partly the result of shifting more F-4s back to the MiGCAP role. Since the beginning of the year Phantoms had flown more strike missions than combat air patrols and while this made up for the attrition rate carving into the available inventory of F-105s, it also lost the F-4 its edge as a fighter, if only momentarily. It came to be seen that a strike configured F-4 flew a wasteful sortie if it could not deliver its ordnance and had instead to jettison its load when NVNAF aircraft intercepted.

In response commanders sent out a flight of F-4s sandwiched between the lead flight of Thunderchiefs and the one following, and also positioned a flight of fighter Phantoms in trail, behind the main strike force elements. As a result May recorded the destruction of 26 MiGs for only two F-4s lost in 72 encounters between the NVNAF and USAF and USN aircraft. F-105s contributed to the score but the lion's share fell to Phantoms on MiGCAP barrier patrols covering Thunderchief strikes.

On 4 May the 8th TFW provided two flights of F-4Cs as MiGCAP for five 355th TFW flights of F-105s. The rear flight was led by Colonel Robin Olds, with First Lieutenant William Lafever as his rear-seater; the other Phantom flight was located at a mid position in the strike force.

Prior to reaching the target the strike force was attacked by two MiG-21s. Picking the last flight of F-105s the enemy fighters were sighted approaching from eleven o'clock. Olds' encounter report told what happened next: 'The MiGs were at my ten o'clock position and closing on Drill flight (the F-l05s) from their 7.30 position. I broke the rear flight into the MiGs, called the F-105s to break, and manoeuvred to obtain a missile firing position on one of the MiG-21s. I obtained a boresight lock-on, interlocks in, went full system, kept the pipper on the MiG, and fired two AIM-7s in a ripple. One AIM-7 went ballistic. The other guided but passed behind the MiG and did not detonate.

'Knowing that I was then too close for further AIM-7 firing, I manoeuvred to obtain AIM-9 firing parameters. The MiG-21 was manoeuvring violently and firing position was difficult to achieve. I snapped two AIM-9s at the MiG and did not observe either missile. The MiG then reversed and presented the best parameter yet. I achieved a loud growl, tracked and fired one AIM-9. From the moment of launch, it was obvious that the missile was locked-on. It guided straight for the MiG and exploded about five to ten feet [1.5-3 m] beneath his tailpipe.

Busy Ubon flightline shows 497th TFS F-4Cs armed for a strike mission; multiple and triple ejector ranks enhanced the F-4's ordnance load significantly. *(MacSorley via Pennick)*

'The MiG went into a series of frantic turns, some of them so violent that the aircraft snap rolled in the opposite direction. Fire was coming from the tailpipe, but I was not sure whether it was normal afterburner, or damage induced. I fired the remaining AIM-9 at one point, but the shot was down toward the ground and the missile did not discriminate. I followed the MiG as he turned south-east and headed for Phuc Yen. The aircraft ceased manoeuvring and went in a straight slant for the airfield. I stayed 2,500 ft [760 m] behind him and observed a brilliant white fire streaming from the left side of his fuselage. It looked like magnesium burning with particles flaking off.

'I had to break off to the right as I neared Phuc Yen runway at about 2,000 ft [610 m], due to heavy, accurate 85 mm barrage (fire). I lost sight of the MiG at that point. Our number three saw the MiG continue in a straight gentle dive and impact approximately 100 yards [91 m] south of the runway.'

Olds continued on into the target area and provided cover for the last of the 355th's strike aircraft as they left. Leading his Phantoms home, Olds dodged two SAMs and spotted five MiG-17s over Hoa Lac airfield. The F-4s joined the MiGs' pattern and circled with them at varying altitudes from 6,000 ft down to 1,500 ft (1,830-460 m), right over the airfield. But before any combat occurred the F-4s had to break off what might have been a profitable engagement and head out, low on fuel.

On 13 May the USAF mounted strikes against the railway yards at Yen Vien and army barracks at Vinh Yen by F-105s with 8th Wing F-4s providing MiGCAP. Having recently been modified to carry Sidewinders, the F-105Ds gave a good account of themselves — no less than five MiG-17s were shot down by 'Thuds', two of them with AIM-9s. This spectacular success was crowned by two more

53

kills by Phantoms, the F-4C crewed by Major William Kirk and First Lieutenant Stephen Wayne getting one with an AIM-9 and that flown by Lieutenant *Colonel* Commander Fred Haeffner and First Lieutenant Michael Bever downing their MiG with a Sparrow. Both crews were from the Wolfpack's 433rd TFS although Haeffner was at that time on a one-week TDY exchange with the 8th TFW and actually assigned to the 390th TFS, 366th TFW. His big MiG victory was credited to the 8th rather than the 366th Wing.

The Phantom crews watched the air battle between the F-105s and MiGs. Immediately they saw a 'Thud' in trouble, Kirk and Wayne waded into the mêlée accompanied by their number two. Aircraft three and four kept high cover. Kirk observed two MiG-17s firing at an F-105 in a hard left turn. The 'Thud' reversed underneath and dived for the deck; the MiGs started to reverse but then pulled up and started left-turning again. Kirk switched his AIM-9 battery to heat mode, obtained a good tone and fired two. The first one tracked well and exploded about 30 ft (9 m) behind one of the enemy fighters which started a very tight left diving spiral turn. There seemed little chance that the MiG could recover as it was on fire from the trailing edge of the left wing to the tail section. Kirk and Wayne lost sight of it as it fell away below the Phantom.

Many Phantoms flew thousands of hours in Vietnam and were passed from one squadron to another over a period of time. This F-4C *63-7668* Georgie Girl of the 497th appears to have been on loan from the 555th during the summer of '67. *(R. Burgess via Pennick)*

Not too long afterwards, '668 was repainted in Triple Nickel codes and had its paintwork generally tidied up. Here it is parked on the ramp at Ubon next to a Thai C-47. *(Burgess via Pennick)*

Kirk loosed off another Sidewinder at two more MiG-17s that came within range, but without a tone, the missile went wide. A third MiG was then attacked with a Sparrow — but both missile and intended quarry disappeared in cloud.

Fred Haeffner and Michael Bever flying aircraft three observed Kirk's successful Sidewinder attack just before they themselves dived down to assist an F-105 with two MiGs chasing him. Attempting to fire two AIM-7s from an overhead position, Haeffner inadvertently fired off three: the first failed to guide and missed the MiG by about 100 ft (30 m). The second missile dropped below the F-4's nose and was temporarily lost to the sight of the crew but it reappeared and both men saw it hit the MiG just behind the canopy. Major Ronald Catton saw the effect: 'The MiG seemed to blow up on the spot; the second missile powdered the MiG; it broke up into many disorganised pieces'.

The following day, 14 May, saw three more MiG-17 kills by Phantoms of the 366th TFW, two of them to gunfire from the SUU-16 pod. Six went down on 20 May, two being the victims of the 366th and four falling to Wolfpack aircraft.

During this period dogfights occurred daily as the US strike forces pounded North Vietnamese targets. For four days results had been inconclusive but on the 20th the Phantom MiGCAP stirred up a hornet's nest while covering an attack on the Kinh No motor vehicle repair yards. The 366th TFW came home with two MiG-21s to its credit while the 8th Wing had to be content with four MiG 17s. The

Wolfpack F-4Cs had the job of MiGCAP for an F-105 raid on the Bac Le railway yards. One flight was positioned in line abreast with the second Thunderchief flight while the remaining F-4 flight was high and to the right of the last flight of 'Thuds'. In support was an EB-66 together with an Iron Hand SAM suppression flight of F-105s. This formidable force swept in from the Gulf of Tonkin and the F-4 crews punched off their centreline tanks as they crossed the group of islands off the coast of North Vietnam. Penetrating inland, the force was about twenty miles (32 km) east of Kep airfield in Route Pack VIB when two SAMs were fired. The Iron Hand flight immediately went into action and struck the missile launch site with Shrike ARMs, causing the SA-2s to lose guidance and present little further threat to the strike force.

Then came a MiG warning, fifteen miles (24 km) from the target. Plans to split the MiGCAP into two, one each to cover sections of F-105s heading for two different targets in the rail yards, were disrupted as each flight of Phantoms detected MiGs. A huge dogfight developed for the next twelve to fourteen minutes with the eight F-4s battling up to fourteen MiGs. The F-l05s pressed on to their target, running the gauntlet of AAA fire but grateful that the MiGs which had been sent up to intercept them were otherwise engaged.

Aircraft Commander Major John Pardo with First Lieutenant Stephen Wayne as back seat pilot, accounted for the first MiG-17. Pardo saw four turning in behind the F-105s. He reported later: 'Colonel Olds fired one missile and told me to 'go get him'. I launched one Sparrow which did not guide. I then launched one Sidewinder which guided and struck the number four MiG.'

Breaking to avoid the attention of other MiGs coming in on him from eight o'clock, Pardo saw his kill burning on the ground in the area below which he had scored the hit. He fired more AAMs but could not observe any results due to having to take fast evasive action as the air battle hotted up.

Two more MiGs fell to the master — Colonel Robin Olds flying with First Lieutenant Croker that day added his third and fourth victories to make him the leading MiG killer in South East Asia. It looked as though the ace from World War 2 who had missed air combat in Korea would succeed again in Vietnam . . .

Olds called the 20 May tangle with MiGs 'quite a remarkable air battle . . . an exact replica of the dogfights in World War 2'. His combat report fully described the action, in graphic terms: 'Our flights of F-4s piled into the MiGs like a sledgehammer, and for about a minute and a half or two minutes that was the most confused, vicious dogfight I have ever been in. There were eight F-4Cs, twelve MiG-17s and one odd flight of F-105s on their way out from the target, who flashed through the battle area.

'Quite frankly, there was not only danger from the guns of the MiGs, but the ever-present danger of a collision to contend with. We went round and round that day with the battles lasting twelve to fourteen minutes, which is a long time. This particular day we found that the MiGs went into a defensive circle low down, about 500 to 1,000 ft [150-305 m]. In the middle of this circle, there were two or three MiGs circling at about a hundred feet [30 m] — sort of in figure-eight patterns. The MiGs were in small groups of two, three, and sometimes four, in a very wide circle. Each time we went in to engage one of these groups, a group on the opposite side of the circle would go full power, pull across the circle, and be in

Thailand's hot and humid climate faded and weathered aircraft camouflage finishes, creating a need for constant repainting if time allowed. This F-4C (63-683), additionally scuffed by flight and ground crew footwear, contrasts sharply with a 'clean' sister ship. *(Burgess via Pennick)*

firing position on our tails almost before we could get into firing position with our missiles. This is very distressing, to say the least.

'The first MiG I lined up was in a gentle left turn, range about 7,000 ft [2,130 m]. My pilot achieved a boresight lock-on, went full system, narrow gate, interlocks in. One of the two Sparrows fired in a ripple guided true and exploded near the MiG. My pilot saw the MiG erupt in flames and go down to the left.

'We attacked again and again, trying to break up that defensive wheel. Finally, once again, fuel consideration necessitated departure. As I left the area by myself, I saw that lone MiG still circling and so I ran out about ten miles [16 km] and said that even if I ran out of fuel, he is going to know he was in a fight.

'I got down on the deck, about fifty feet [15 m], and headed right for him. I don't think he saw me for quite a while. But when he did, he went mad — twisting, turning, dodging and trying to get away. I kept my speed down so I wouldn't overrun him and I stayed behind him. He headed up a narrow little valley to a low ridge of hills. I knew he was either going to hit that ridge up ahead or pop over the ridge to save himself. The minute he popped over I was going to get him with a Sidewinder.

'I fired one AIM-9 which did not track and the MiG pulled up over a ridge, turned left, and gave me a dead astern shot. I obtained a good growl. I fired from about 25 to 50 feet [8-15 m] off the grass and he was clear of the ridge by only another 50 to 100 feet [15-30 m] when the Sidewinder caught him.

'The missile tracked and exploded 5 to 10 feet [1.5-3 m] to the right side of the aft fuselage. The MiG spewed pieces and broke hard left and down from about 200 feet (60 m). I overshot and lost sight of him.

'I was quite out of fuel and all out of missiles and pretty deep in enemy territory all by myself, so it was high time to leave. We learned quite a bit from this fight. We learned you don't pile into these fellows with eight airplanes all at once. You are only a detriment to yourself.'

The final MiG-17 destroyed in the 20 May battle went to the lead aircraft of the first F-4 flight crewed by Major Philip Combies and First Lieutenant Daniel Lafferty. It was Combies' second victory. Having engaged several MiGs without results he was climbing to rejoin the battle when he saw a MiG-17 in hot pursuit of a Phantom about 1½ miles away. The F-4 was that of Robin Olds, who, realising he was being pursued, broke hard left. The MiG overshot and headed out towards Kep airfield about eight miles (13 km) distant. Combies overhauled him and obtained a good AIM-9 tone. He fired. The missile impacted in the MiG's tailpipe area and it caught fire. From 1,500 ft (460 m) the enemy machine went 'belly up' and flipped over into a dive. It did not recover and was seen to impact by Combies and Lafferty.

More MiGs fell on 22 May and 3 June but it was on 5 June that the Wolfpack scored its next success. Major Everett T. Raspberry, Jr, and Captain Francis M. Gullick of the Triple Nickel squadron downed a MiG-17 with an AIM-7 in the first recorded victory for the F-4D and the first of three kills for the day. Two of them went to the 8th Wing.

Again the Phantoms were on MiGCAP for Iron Hand 'Thuds'; Raspberry and Gullick countered a MiG-17 intercept on the F-105 formation, manoeuvring with their wingman against seven or eight enemy fighters in a wagon wheel formation.

Setting up a small ruse, the Phantoms turned with the MiGs several times then disengaged, flying south-east for some four miles (6.5 km). They then turned back into the MiGs. Raspberry and Gullick set up a MiG spotted at twelve o'clock high for an AIM-4 shot. The Falcon missed, having failed to guide.

Disengaging once more, Raspberry turned back a second time and came in low. Obtaining radar lock-on for an AIM-7 shot at a MiG in his eleven o'clock position Raspberry was annoyed to see another miss. 'On my third approach to the MiGs I was between 500 and 1,000 feet [150-305 m] on a north-westerly heading. I could see three — one in my twelve o'clock, slightly high and two more in my eleven o'clock position, slightly low.'

Then, Raspberry reported, 'My GIB locked onto a target which was obviously one of the MiGs I had seen in my eleven o'clock position as I turned slightly left and down to centre the steering dot. I observed the rate of closure to be 900 knots. When the ASE circle was maximum diameter, I fired an AIM-7.

'The missile appeared to be headed straight for the oncoming MiG. I was unable to watch the impact because Colonel Olds (flying lead in an adjacent flight) called me to break right as a MiG was in my four o'clock and firing. My wingman, Captain Douglas Cairns, was unable to see the AIM-7 as it approached the MiG and observed the MiG as it struck the ground. I would estimate the MiG's altitude at the time of impact as 100-300 ft [30-90 m].'

Awaiting the next call and its necessary warload, a Night Owls F-4C *63-7710* bakes under the Thai sunshine. *(Burgess via Pennick)*

A second MiG fell to a 366th TFW Phantom and a few minutes later Captains Richard Pascoe and Norman Wells knocked down another. Flying wing to Colonel Olds, Pascoe and Wells had scored before — indeed Pascoe was actually a Major by the time of the 5 June sortie but had not at that time 'put up the gold leaves'.

Their action came as Olds' flight covered the egress of the F-105s from the target area. Monitoring radio chatter from a fight involving 'Thuds', MiGs and a 366th TFW element which included MiG killers Majors Durwood, Priester and Captain John Pankhurst, Olds and Pascoe reversed course and went back to help out. Pascoe saw MiGs flying in flights and singly, manoeuvring with the other US aircraft, high up at nine and three o'clock. Both Olds and Pascoe pursued a MiG orbiting at nine o'clock while Phantoms number three and four in the flight took care of those seen in the three o'clock sector.

Olds, having expended all his AIM-4 and AIM-7 missiles without effect, passed the lead to Dick Pascoe: 'I picked up a single MiG-17 at approximately five nautical miles in front of us. I fired two AIM-9s as the MiG started a slight climb and observed the first to impact at the extreme tail end and the second about three feet [1 m] up the fuselage from the tail. The MiG continued in his left descending turn and struck the ground as the canopy was seen to leave the aircraft. The aircraft was totally destroyed.

Low drag Snakeye bombs and Sparrows on a 497th F-4C (*63-7594*) with a later production model, *64-785*, alongside. *(Burgess via Pennick)*

Olds and his back-seater, First Lieutenant James Thibodeaux, saw their wingman's Sidewinders impact the MiG, reporting that the pilot ejected just before it crashed 'in a large fireball'.

On 23 August an F-105D shot down another MiG-17 to end the US run of kills for the summer 1967 period. For nearly two months the NVNAF seldom ventured out and US losses were slight as the enemy initiated another round of training to replace those aircraft and pilots they had lost. Defence was momentarily left to SAMs and AAA, more than able to take a heavy toll of the attackers. Not that air combat did not take place during September and October — it was merely, as had happened on so many occasions before, that the Americans were unable to record victories. The 23 August mission to Yen Vien rail yards saw the North Vietnamese come off best. Early in the mission, two MiG-21s destroyed a pair of F-4s with AAMs before a giant dogfight developed. In the confusing mêlée an F-4C crew fired at what they thought was a MiG but was actually an F-4D. Luckily the mistake was rectified in time by the Aircraft Commander who told his back-seater to break lock. Both AIM-7s went ballistic as soon as the lock-on was broken and no damage was done. The crew flying the would-be victim Phantom carried on, unaware of the hectic efforts to avoid giving them a nasty surprise . . .

Both the downed F-4s were from the 8th TFW and two more F-4s were lost, one to flak and one through running out of fuel when it could not reach a tanker in time. Robin Olds was annoyed at being surprised by the MiG-21s — and furious when he found out that US intelligence had known beforehand that the enemy was changing his tactics following recent heavy losses.

Knowing that they were unlikely to come off best against a fully alerted Phantom force, the NVNAF resorted to approaching US strike forces at low level, climbing fast to altitude and then making a long dive, culminating in a single firing pass before running for home, either their own bases or sanctuary airfields in China.

Olds' rage was understandable; had he known what sort of attack he was likely to encounter he would have deployed his forces differently. He said, 'I would have split my MiGCAP element up; three and four would have accelerated below the strike force and ingressed 10-15 miles [16-24 km] ahead of them. My wingman and I would have turned easterly toward Thud Ridge prior to the strike force . . . accelerated . . . gained 15-20 miles [24-32 km] separation . . . and swooped over the force as they turned south-easterly down the ridge. The GCI controller would already have picked us up on radar; he would have observed our turn. I'll bet one hundred dollars that he'd have called off the MiGs. He probably would have said, 'Break, break, they're on you'. Then we would have turned in behind the strike force and continued ingress.'

That Olds' wing had not been alerted due to the tortuous chain of command was all too typical of the system that was running the war. On the one hand the higher echelons would make almost microscopic analysis of gun camera film, eye-witness accounts and combat reports whenever a US fighter pilot claimed a victory — yet not pass on vital information regarding enemy tactics. No fighter pilot worth his salt was afraid to face heavy odds even if the enemy did not play things 'by the book' — the name of the game was after all, the art of the stab in the back, the surprise attack, chopping down the enemy before he had a chance to get you. But it was quite another thing to waste good crews and expensive aircraft through faulty intelligence.

# Chapter 8
# More MiGs fall

Although Lieutenant General William Momyer was moved to comment after the summer fighter victories that 'we have driven the MiGs out of the sky for all practical purposes', air combat over North Vietnam was far from over. Momyer's report was made to a Senate sub-committee on 16 August, before a change of NVNAF tactics marked a renewed round of air combat, albeit on a smaller scale. Over-optimism about the progress of the war and what the United States was achieving had been voiced many times before, but there was still no tangible proof that North Vietnam was willing to negotiate a peace settlement.

The tempo of the war did not decrease and USAF and Navy aircraft continued to mount air strikes on North Vietnam's industrial power base and military installations. Gradually, the 'no go' areas imposed on US pilots were removed. Six months into 1967 the 'out country' war over North Vietnam had seen more realistic broadening of the target list to include the airfields at Kep, Hoa Lac, Kien An and Phuc Yen. Only Gia Lam, Hanoi's international airport was spared. On 20 July Rolling Thunder objectives were increased by sixteen more fixed targets and 23 additional road, rail and waterway links inside the Hanoi-Haiphong restricted area, all of which assisted the North Vietnamese to marshal and direct forces and material for infiltration south via the notorious Ho Chi Minh Trail. Rarely were these targets put permanently out of action; immense efforts by the Vietnamese repaired or bypassed shattered lines of communication so that the men and supplies kept rolling. Denied the chance to bomb or mine Haiphong Harbour, US airpower could do little to cut off Russian and Chinese supplies at source.

For all US forces the Vietnam war was, however, an invaluable training ground for new equipment and tactics, with the Army and particularly the Air Force reaping the greatest benefits through modernisation of force structure and equipment and laying the foundation of a rapid deployment force. In the first of the truly modern wars innovations were made which were to radically alter the way in which the United States — and other Western nations — were to prepare for any future conflict.

As the spearhead of the Air Force (notwithstanding the early deployment of the F-111 on a limited basis which returned good and bad results) the F-4 was the most modern aircraft to see action and it was not surprising that many of the technical advances were tailored to this one type. Together with its sister Wings based in Thailand, the 8th TFW would prove numerous new ideas as the Vietnam

'Ripchord' was the name applied to F-4C *63-629* of the 433rd. Well loaded with drop tanks, rocket pods and a centreline gun, it was seen at Da Nang in August 1967. *(Neil Schneider via Pennick)*

war entered its latter stages — just how sound the Phantom's 'multi-role' concept had been was being made abundantly clear under combat conditions.

Probably the greatest step forward to emerge from the air war over the North was the need for an efficient method of detecting and neutralising surface-to-air missiles, arguably the greatest threat to tactical strike forces. Although the SA-2 Guideline SAM and its Fan Song radar and guidance system hardly represented the latest state-of-the-art, extensive use of both in defending important North Vietnamese targets made effective countermeasures of paramount importance.

Wild Weasel rapidly became the generic term for aircraft equipped to find and destroy SAMs, and the USAF had by the mid-1960s achieved a good deal, firstly with adaptations of the F-100 Super Sabre followed by the F-105F. Both types saw extensive action and in the main, were highly successful in reducing the SAM threat. But neither type was ideal; the F-100F lacked performance and range and the two-seat Thunderchief, while a far more able platform had drawbacks, not the least of which was the fact that any losses could not be replaced from current production. It was therefore logical to adapt the F-4 to the Wild Weasel role. Work began on the F-4C in 1967. It was expected that the first aircraft so modified would fly some six months after that of the first Wild Weasel F-105F in January 1966, but it was to be 1968 before everyone was satisfied that the Phantom could be modified to undertake the task satisfactorily.

A crew training programme was also initiated at Nellis AFB and among the first graduates from Wild Weasel college were the highly experienced crews who had previously flown the F-4 over Vietnam, with one or more combat tours behind them. The training programme progressed, while aircraft modifications lagged. After having completed a year at Nellis, men such as Dick Pascoe and Norman Wells left for SE Asia to join, in their case the 8th TFW, without the aircraft they had been trained to use. Wild Weasel Class IVA and IVB lasted so long that the Air Force had no choice but to transfer the graduates or assign them permanently to Nellis. Pascoe and Wells were among the fourteen F-4 crewmen who completed the initial courses and, flying not Weasel F-4Cs but standard aircraft, promptly became MiG killers — in fact seven individuals scored victories and three of them shot down two each.

Work progressed under the programme designation Wild Weasel IV-C and after approximately twelve months of frustration McDonnell engineers embarked on revising installation of the various antennae, electronics and associated wiring to enable the F-4C to detect enemy radar and destroy it with anti-radiation missiles. This work, even under top priority conditions, was not to bear fruit until late 1969.

In the meantime, the war against North Vietnam went on. Robin Olds relinquished command of the 8th Wing at Ubon on 30 September 1967, handing over to Colonel Robert V. Spencer, who actually occupied the CO's office from the 23rd. In his tenure as Wing Commander Robin Olds had brought the 8th TFW to a high peak of efficiency, putting it well on the way to becoming the top MiG-killing tactical fighter wing in SE Asia.

Among the electronic equipment developed to defeat enemy air defences was the ALQ-131 ECM pod, here fitted to a 33rd TFW F-4. *(USAF)*

Another of the 8th Wing's MiG killers was F-4C *64-838*, seen here with 433rd TFS codes.
*(MacSorley via Pennick)*

While Olds was in command, the 8th Wing received the first of three Presidential Unit Citations it was to be awarded during Vietnam operations. All were for sustained periods of operations, the first PUC covering the period 16 December 1966 to 2 January 1967. The Wing also received a number of campaign streamers during the period, and was awarded a total of sixteen by the end of the war. Streamers covered all the major phases of the Vietnam air war or served to highlight an individual unit's contribution to campaigns-within-campaigns, of which there were many.

Among the early innovations introduced in Vietnam to make life a little easier for tactical aircrew had been the College Eye airborne early warning system on the EC-121 Constellation. This was enhanced in August 1967 by Rivet Top, a radar watch also accommodated by the ubiquitous Connie. Gradually broadening its monitoring and control over the entire tactical air spectrum of North Vietnam since the first deployment in the spring of 1965 with five EC-121s, the detachment of the 552nd Airborne Early Warning and Control Wing from McClellan AFB, California, became a vital element of air operations. In conjuction with the USAF control centre at Da Nang, College Eye/Rivet Top aircraft orbited the Gulf of Tonkin and other locations to provide total coverage of the operational area up to the Chinese border. In 1967 the service was broadened not only to warn incoming Air Force flights of imminent MiG attack, but to actively direct MiGCAP F-4 flights onto MiGs as they took off.

Combat action for the 8th TFW hotted up in May 1967, no fewer than seven MiGs falling to Phantoms. All but one of the enemy aircraft were MiG-17s and all victories went to crews flying the F-4C. Only Robin Olds shot down a MiG-21. Having apparently recovered some of their aggressiveness following the beating received during the ruse missions of January, the North Vietnamese Air Force again rose to challenge US incursions into its airspace.

The temporary lull, enforced on the enemy not only by losses but also by the north-east monsoon, saw low-key activity through February and March. Weather considerations also forced some curtailment of US air operations during the period. But when conditions allowed, the NVNAF ventured out, mainly to provide standing patrols over their bases. Attacks on US strike forces were still largely on a random basis, usually as they entered or left the target area. MiG-21s occasionally made quick and potentially dangerous hit and run passes but overall the effort seemed uncoordinated and on too small a scale to be really effective.

F-105s shot down the first MiG-17s to fall victim in aerial combat for two months when gradually improving weather produced a number of skirmishes in March. April's days were clearer and the US pressed home another round of strikes on targets in the North with renewed vigour. The effectiveness of these, partly aided by weapons of increased accuracy, hurt North Vietnamese war-making potential — there was bound, sooner or later, to be a spirited response from the NVNAF. The F-105 successes of April were continued through the early part of May as Rolling Thunder V, beginning on 14 February and destined to last until 24 December, recorded a new peak in air actions.

Despite the official view of knocking down enemy MiGs, eager fighter pilots often saw this one yardstick as a measure of their prowess in combat; for some it became the raison d'être for flying over North Vietnam, with hauling bombs definitely relegated to second place. It was then with some elation that October 1967 saw a renewal of American success over the NVNAF, following the solitary kill made in August by a 388th TFW F-105. It was high time the leading MiG killing wing added to its score.

An F-105 also scored the first victory of the month when on the 18th a

As Ubon was a Royal Thai Air Force base, the Wolfpack's F-4s often shared dispersals with that country's T-28s, Sabres and other types. This F-4C of the 433rd was pictured in the summer of '67 with RTAF T-28s in the background. *(Burgess via Pennick)*

En route back from a mission, F-4C *63-7710* of the 497th TFS was lost on 12 June 1967, some six months after shooting down a MiG-21 during Operation Bolo. *(MacSorley)*

Thunderchief of the 355th Wing clobbered a MiG-17 with 20-mm gunfire. A week later the Wolfpack's Major William Kirk and First Lieutenant Theodore Bongartz shot down a MiG-21 during a strike that was calculated to bring enemy fighters to combat — the target was Phuc Yen, the largest MiG base in North Vietnam.

The USAF put up four separate strike force elements drawn from three Wings and the results were excellent. All bombs fell in the target area and no US aircraft were lost. Mission planners had to calculate some losses from each strike on the North and Phuc Yen carried an estimated three per cent loss ratio. Not only were the estimates wrong but the opposition lost a valuable MiG-21 into the bargain, plus four more on the ground. The bombs also destroyed four MiG-17s and badly damaged a MiG-15, used by the NVNAF for training.

The aerial kill took place during the initial attack; William Kirk noted how different this victory was compared to his first when he got a MiG-17 with an AAM in one pass. The contest with the MiG-21 turned into an old-fashioned duel in true dogfighting tradition, lasting some time.

Timely warning of enemy air activity was passed to the US force as it crossed into North Vietnam, indicating that MiGs could be expected at their six o'clock position, about eight miles (13 km) distant. Kirk and Bongartz flying MiGCAP element lead noted that the warning was right on the money and turned back into the enemy intercept path. Coming out of a 180 degree turn, pilot Bongartz acquired a lock-on to a target 30 degrees to the right of the F-4, four miles (6.5 km) out. Visual identification confirmed that it was a MiG-21.

Climbing, the MiG was pursued by the Phantom; it rolled and dived, then made several hard manoeuvring turns. The US crew thought that the pilot had by then decided to extricate himself from the combat, as the MiG continually sought the cover of available cloud. Achieving a good AIM-7 tone, the F-4 crew launched two. One exploded close to their quarry but the second Sparrow's flightpath went unseen. There was no visible damage to the enemy fighter so the F-4 closed to between 500 and 700 ft (150-213 m) to set up a gunnery pass. A stream of high explosive incendiary shells hit the MiG's fuselage between the wing roots and pieces were seen to fly off, seconds before it was engulfed in flames.

Kirk and Bongartz saw the pilot bale out as the MiG-21 rolled to the right and crashed after a fifteen degree dive. The F-4 turned and flew close to the enemy pilot hanging under his parachute — but he turned away. Neither of the Americans saw what he looked like . . . Two days later the 8th Wing's 555th TFS scored three more kills, one of which was the first of five kills Phantoms were to score with the AIM-4 during the conflict.

On 26 October all the kills went to members of a single MiGCAP flight covering a reconnaissance sortie. Somewhat rashly, six MiG-17s took on four F-4Ds. They bounced the Americans three miles north-west of Phuc Yen airfield; the recon aircraft immediately took its leave and the Phantoms went to work.

First to score was Captain John Logeman, Jr, and First Lieutenant Frederick McCoy, in the lead Phantom. Seeing the MiGs climbing about six miles before they reached Phuc Yen, Logeman called his flight to turn into them:

'As I completed my right turn, heading approximately 090 degrees at 17,000 ft [5,180 m], I placed the pipper on the lead MiG-17 and fired two AIM-7E missiles in boresight mode. The first missile did not guide. The second came up into the reticule and appeared to be on a collision course with the MiG. We were head-on at this time and his cannons were firing. I pulled up to avoid the cannon fire and did not observe missile detonation. I immediately turned hard left to re-engage the MiGs on a west heading. During this left turn I observed a parachute in the area of intended missile impact and a MiG-17 was descending inverted, trailing sparks from the fuselage.'

Major John Hall and First Lieutenant Albert Hamilton, in aircraft two, saw the parachute, by which time a second MiG-17 was attacking Logeman. Coming in on the Phantom from ten o'clock, it then turned away at about two miles (3.2 m) range — not a very wise move. McCoy obtained a full system lock-on and Logeman selected two AIM-7Es. One failed to leave the aircraft but the second one streaked away and appeared to be guiding correctly. The result was unobserved as Logeman and McCoy had to manoeuvre away from another MiG-17 making a cannon attack from their seven o'clock position.

Phantom number three was crewed by Captain William Gordon III and First Lieutenant James Monsees, and their victory came minutes after Logeman's. Watching the MiGs attack from his three o'clock sector, Gordon turned his element to take them on. But he was too close to use AAMs. He disengaged, gained lateral separation and set up another attack. With two MiG-17s in the pipper, Gordon's pilot got a boresight full system lock-on. But again the reliability of the Sparrow was disappointing. Only one fired. What happened to it was unseen by either man as another MiG was attacking.

Having disengaged again, Gordon reversed back into the action — and found a pilot under a white 'chute in the approximate position he had fired the Sparrow, at 16,000 ft (4,877 m) altitude. Breaking away twice more to find a favourable firing position, Gordon and Monsees tried for a tail shot, selecting an AIM-4D. Having cooled the Falcon prior to launch, Gordon obtained a tone and fired it on self-track. He had full system lock-on at a range of about 6,000 ft (1,830 m). Again having to break away from an enemy fighter, Gordon did not see the Falcon impact although it appeared to guide accurately for the MiG-17 he had selected. A second 'chute was then seen, at 8,000 ft (2,438 m).

Captains Larry Cobb and Alan Lavoy were flying the number four Phantom and were the last crew to score a kill. Flying wing to Gordon and Monsees, they stuck with the number three until Gordon separated the first time and then re-entered the battle. Having fired a missile on the way through the dogfight, Cobb exited on the other side, saw the first chute and streaked back into the mêlée, continuing to do this until a suitable target presented itself. On what would have to be the last pass due to their fuel state Cobb and Lavoy picked up two MiG-17s at ten o'clock. Again an AIM-4D was selected and with self-track lock-on, a single round was fired. Cobb's combat report rounded off with the result of the action: 'I observed the AIM-4D impact on the tail of the MiG-17, and he exploded and started to roll right. At this time the pilot ejected and his plane spiralled earthward in flames.'

Clean ejector racks and missile bays mean a break in operations for these F-4Cs, including the 497th's 63-7552. (*Burgess via Pennick*)

A photographic specialist inserting the rearwards facing strike camera in the nose cone of an F-4D. These cameras often recorded the behaviour of ordnance as it fell away from the aircraft and helped overcome any malfunctions, it not being unknown for circuit shorts to cause everything, including the racks, to jettison at once. *(USAF)*

On 27 October a further F-105 victory over a MiG-17 made USAF planners wonder if the NVNAF would now be forced to initiate another stand-down period, considering its recent losses on the ground and in the air. But numerous sanctuary areas available to the enemy resulted in a continuing round of air combat in the weeks leading up to Christmas 1967. Those fighters which had been moved back to China when the US began to bomb their forward airfields had, it seemed, returned and American crews did not see a significant reduction in the number of interceptors during a period in which they mounted strikes on every jet-capable airfield north of the 20th parallel, but still excluding Gia Lam.

Two more MiG-17s were shot down by the 8th Wing on 6 November, both being the victims of 20 mm gunfire from the aircraft of Captain Darrell Simmonds and First Lieutenant George McKinney of the 435th TFS, which provided the MiGCAP to strikes on Kep. As it was the only one, it had to split in order to cover the F-105 flights which in turn divided to bomb the airfield and nearby rail yards. With no warnings of enemy aircraft on the run in to the targets, the 'Thuds' were able to release their loads without interference from that quarter: it was as the first strike flights were exiting the target that the MiGs struck. The MiGCAP turned south to engage them, but failed to make visual contact. A turn to the north-east then located a flight of MiG-17s as the F-4s came ninety degrees to the egressing F-105 force on a beam heading. Intent on the last of the departing 'Thuds', the MiG pilots appeared not to detect the Phantoms rapidly closing in on them.

One MiG had opened fire — but the pilot rapidly stopped firing to take evasive action when he saw what was coming at him . . . Simmonds and McKinney threw the Phantom into several turns to get within gun range. Closing to 1,500 ft (457 m), Simmonds fired. Shells struck the aft section of the MiG which burst into flames. Jettisoning his canopy, the Red pilot rode his stricken fighter down, only managing to bale out just before the Phantom crew saw it hit. As his aircraft disappeared in an orange fireball, the pilot was lost to sight in trees.

Turning his flight back towards the briefed egress route, Simmonds and McKinney picked up a lone MiG-17 at four o'clock heading away at low level. Seeing the F-4 coming up on him the MiG pilot dropped 200 ft (60 m) and flew

More evidence of dual ownership on F-4C 63-7580 which also has a white-painted intake aft of the nose radome, a favoured location for aircraft nicknames. *(Burgess via Pennick)*

into a valley. Close behind, the Phantom was ready for any evasive move; it came as the MiG broke hard left and climbed. This enabled the Phantom pilot to track him accurately and at 1,000 ft (305 m) he opened fire. The MiG-17 exploded and fell to earth in pieces.

One more MiG-17 was to fall to the Wolfpack before the end of 1967, again succumbing to the lethal stream of bullets from the F-4D's belly gun pod — but on this occasion the enemy aircraft was destroyed by two guns, as the Phantom shared the kill with an F-105F. This meant under the prevailing score system that the four crewman each received a half credit even though only one aircraft was actually shot down. For the 8th Wing crew, Major Joseph Moore and George McKinney, this represented the only half credit to be awarded to the Wolfpack during hostilities.

Tactically, the 19 December strike on the Viet Tri and Tien Cuong was a small victory for the North Vietnamese, as early interception prevented half the force from bombing. Jettisoning their loads in order to manoeuvre in combat, the F-105s evened things up by adding one complete kill to their half-score.

As 1967 passed into history the USAF had completed the staggering total of 176,000 war sorties, an all-time Vietnam war peak and significantly higher than the total of approximately 130,000 for 1966. To deliver a vast tonnage of ordnance to North Vietnamese targets had cost 270 Air Force aircraft, the USAF having in its turn destroyed 59 MiGs in aerial combat plus 19 more during strikes on NVNAF airfields.

While the bombing had undoubtedly hurt enemy war support facilities, disrupted urban life, tied up thousands of workers on bomb damage repair and caused some drain on NVA and Viet Cong troop levels in the South through the need to keep a nucleus of trained personnel to man AAA and SAM sites, there was little tangible evidence that the war against their homeland was cracking the North Vietnamese will to fight and more importantly, defeating them. There appeared to be no way, apart from feeding more crews and aircraft into the strike squadrons in Thailand, of bringing about any conclusion primarily by the use of airpower. Critics observed that the US appeared to be intent on 'bombing North Vietnam back to the stone age', a comment all too familiar to the aircrews who had to do the job, and typical of an overkill media coverage of the war, all too much of which seemed incapable of in-depth analysis.

To their credit the majority of US airmen carried out their exacting task well; while there were mistakes at every level, while bombs did drop in the wrong place — were even targeted on the wrong places — and while the weapons used often proved to be mediocre, in time there arose a widespread feeling that the war (as it was being fought in 1967) was almost unwinnable, although an extreme effort was nearly always made to bomb the briefed targets as accurately as possible. It was for the politicians to decide if the last ton, the last hundred tons or the last ten thousand tons had achieved any goal. Airmen were more preoccupied with how many more tons it would take and how many of their people and aircraft would be at risk in doing the job tomorrow, next week or six months' hence. For some it had already been a very long war . . .

# Chapter 9
# Olds' story

The story of the 8th TFW in Vietnam is always linked with the exploits of Robin Olds — and rightly so. Under the leadership of a man with awesome experience at the controls of a fighter (essentially totalling 46 years) Olds was uniquely qualified to lead a Phantom Wing in Thailand. The assignment was not to everyone's liking but Robin Olds appeared to thrive on the experience and he did as much as most Wing Commanders to weld his team into the highly efficient organisation that it was. Both during and after the war, he wrote and spoke at length on his own view of this modern war in comparison with the conditions he had experienced during World War 2. What comes over in his writing is a balanced, common sense attitude to the job in hand, tempered with observation of what could have been done to make life a little easier for his combat crews, and a healthy regard for the qualities of the enemy. Above all Robin Olds is unstinting in his praise of the men he led. In their turn they knew that with Olds in charge everything that could have been done to make their task possible had been carried out. If it had not been, they also knew that the 'Old Man' would soon want to know the reason why. There follows an overview by Olds, starting with a description of the 11 August 1967 mission to knock out the Paul Doumier Bridge, a tough target well defended by the formidable array of anti-aircraft weapons available to the North Vietnamese.

'The Doumier Bridge carries highway and railroad traffic across the Red River in the north-east section of Hanoi, vital to the movement of war material from Communist China to the North Vietnamese and Viet Cong forces in South Vietnam. The only Red River span within thirty miles [48 km] of Hanoi, it and its approaches are guarded by SAM sites, automatic weapons sites, and more than 100 37 mm, 57 mm and 85 mm anti-aircraft cannon sites. And the entire MiG force is well within range of the target area.

'If we don't knock out the bridge on the first try, the defences probably will get even tighter. It will take pinpoint precision to hit the 38 ft [11.5 m] width of the mile-long [1,800 m] span and not damage the nearby civilian areas.

'My Wolfpack F-4Cs join KC-135 tankers from the 4258th Wing at Takhli and F-105s from Takhli's 355th TFW and Korat's 388th TFW. Colonel Bob White, former X-15 pilot and astronaut, leads the first group, the 355th. Each "Thud" is heavily loaded with one 3,000 lb [1,360 kg] bomb under each wing and a centreline drop tank, instead of the usual six 750-pounders [340 kg] and 450-gallon [2,045 litre] drop tank under each wing. From Ubon to Hanoi, the weather is clear with visibility unlimited all the way.

'Ahead of us are EB-66s, whose job is to identify and jam enemy radar, along with F-105s which will go after the anti-aircraft sites. Behind are RF-101s and RF-4Cs of the 11th and 432nd Tactical Reconnaissance Squadrons. After we've pulled off the target but while the enemy is fully alerted and throwing everything he's got, they'll fly over the bridge at maximum speed and photograph the results.

'As we fly down the Red River toward Hanoi — about thirty miles [48 km] from target — seven SAMs are fired at our F-4s. But we evade them, as well as the heavy AAA fire. Twenty miles [32 km] from the target, four MiGs pass 200 ft [60 m] below the flak suppression force of F-105s but, strangely, don't try to engage them. We and the F-105s keep formation and refuse to jettison our bombs, contrary to the MiGs' wishes. We're frequently glancing over our shoulder at the trailing MiGs, wondering whether we'll have to cut in our afterburners to outrun them.

'Now the flak is even heavier and, as one pilot remarks, "we're trying to run several blocks in a rainstorm without letting a drop hit us". We're engulfed in the black smoke of 85 mm bursts. More SAMs, but there's little point in evasive action against one site only to be hit by another. As the force starts down the bomb run, hundreds of 37 mm and 57 mm guns open up on us. Aircraft are hit but not downed.

Excellent Ubon flight line view of the F-4C in which Col Robin Olds scored his first kill. Serial *63-680* was apparently nicknamed 'Candy' had the blue and yellow rudder stripes described elsewhere, and the little red lion. Subsequent to this photograph the crew chief Frank MacSorley had the 497th's owl insignia applied to it. The aircraft shows both Olds' MiG kill and one scored by another crew. *(via Pennick/Ward)*

'The first group of F-105s is jinking hard off the target and pulling away. We can see their 3,000-pounders walking across the bridge. The centre span falls into the Red River. Now we go in and blast the 85 mm sites. Lieutenant Colonel Harry W. Schurr, leading the third group — the 388th "Thuds" — sees their 3,000-pounders "popping like big orange balls" as they hit the bridge. Another span has been dropped.

'More SAMs narrowly miss the force as we turn hard right, reassemble at Thud Ridge, the best known checkpoint in the air war, and head for the waiting tankers. Every aircraft is recovered safely, although several have taken serious hits.

'The Doumier raid illustrates one of the most unique features of this air war — that fully half of our pilots' concern is with what's coming up from the ground. When you're up in the barrel round Hanoi, it's like flying through the Ruhr in World War 2.

Armament specialists make final adjustments to a Multiple Ejector Rack (MER) [handwritten: *Triple* ... *TER*] carrying low-drag 750lb bombs in a scene re-enacted thousands if not millions of times during the Vietnam war. *(USAF)*

'In that war, you caught hell from the ground if you blundered over a few major, heavily defended target areas. But, generally, the fighter pilot could weave around and not get shot at by the heavy stuff. You got down low, and there was lots of countryside you could fly over and lots of lucrative targets that were relatively lightly defended.

'Not that I am one who holds with the contention that the flak in North Vietnam is thicker than that encountered in Germany. I don't think there's any way to equate the two ground-fire situations.

'In Germany, the 88 mm guns protecting such places as Berlin, Mersberg, Regensburg, Osnabruck and Hamburg were concentrated in great mass. They used to fling up against every slow-moving bomber formation a barrage of flak that blackened the sky for as long as a mile and perhaps a half mile wide.

'It was an absolutely incredible sight. The bombers were moving at something like 220-225 mph [350-360 km/h] ground speed, depending on the wind. The ground gunners had plenty of time to shoot — almost at their leisure. That flak certainly was thicker than anything seen near Hanoi.

'In this war, you don't float around within fifty miles [80 km] or so of Hanoi. Even with external bombs our F-4s are travelling very near the speed of sound. When we roll in on the target, the North Vietnamese have to shoot quickly. The flak up north is said to be worse than Germany's because it is about ten times as accurate. The 85 mm is much more accurate and numerous than the German '88s. For the exposure time, we get a much greater density of flak. Also, all targets are in a relatively condensed area. The enemy can afford the luxury of concentrating his defences in known target areas because, geographically, he's small and doesn't have many major targets.

'Although North Vietnamese ground fire is not as thick as World War 2's it's worse in the sense that it's far more accurate and deadly. You get more thrown at you on every mission up around Hanoi — very impressive, indeed!

'The only way you can go into these heavily defended areas today and get out again is by executing a carefully prepared, well-coordinated plan that every man follows to the letter. You can deviate, but this takes experience. Even if you were allowed to, you would not go in and make an armed reconnaissance on a road north of Hanoi or between Hanoi and Haiphong. This would be sheer stupidity. If you go in and strafe, you'd better be prepared for some pretty high losses. We lost many fighters doing just that in World War 2. In North Vietnam, we don't operate that way.

'You see a MiG coming at you, so you want to ram full power and pull five Gs in a turn away from him. But you don't do that because you could get zapped by a SAM. If you see a SAM and sort of split-S down to the grass, you're out of your ever-lovin' mind because the small-arms fire can get you down there — where the SAMs are trying to force you. The SAMs are a terrible menace, but not a deadly menace, and we have ways of evading them. If you get busted out of formation, you're terribly vulnerable. Two of our F-4s were shot down that way. But even if you do get broken off, your ECM gear will help you against the opposition, such as enemy gun-laying radars on the ground.

'In an area smaller than many of our States the enemy has concentrated innumerable automatic weapons, more than 5,000 anti-aircraft guns, more than 200 SAM sites which have fired more than 5,000 SAMs, and a sizeable MiG force.

Due to its lower numbers, the MiG-21 was less of a threat to US air strikes than the older MiG-17. It did however pack a punch in the form of cannon and heat-seeking Atoll AAMs, two of which are carried by this machine, photographed near Hanoi in late 1966. *(USAF)*

The bombing of the north has forced him to develop a sophisticated and reasonably well integrated air-defence system. We can jam his radar, which sites his guns and tells his MiGs where we are at all times.

'But the less time we spend in his heavily defended areas, the less chance we take of getting clobbered. The problem is to achieve a balance between our capability to do the job and an acceptable survivability rate.

'The MiG pilots are a lot better than the average German pilot towards the end of World War 2. They know their airplanes well and fly them well. When they're turned loose, they're very fierce competitors. More than competitors, they're downright dangerous. Sometimes, when they've forced us to jettison our bombs before reaching the target, we've had to go in and teach them a lesson or chase them out. But our basic job over there is to bomb targets, not chase MiGs. If they happen to get in the way, so much the worse for them. The last dogfight score I recall was 110 MiGs downed to 48 US airplanes. As of May 1967 when I shot down my third and fourth MiGs, 603 US planes had gone down in North Vietnam. As of 24 September 1968, the total stood at 899.

'The MiG-21 really became effective in August 1967. It's a Mach 2 aircraft with both manoeuvrability and excess thrust, despite its single engine. Carrying both missiles and guns, it's versatile. We need a new air-superiority fighter which will be clearly superior to the MiG-21.

'I could go up today in a P-51 and wrestle with those MiGs and they'd never touch me. But I might not touch them either. So I get something much better than the MiG-17, like an F-4. But now I have to touch the '17 very carefully. If I try to fight his kind of fight, I'm in deep trouble. He's going to zap me.

'Air-to-air missiles gave our fighters a tremendous capability compared to the MiG-17, which carries only cannon and rockets. But fighting a MiG with a gunless F-4 is like fighting a guy with a dagger when he's got a sword, or maybe vice versa. A fighter without a gun, which is the most versatile air-to-air weapon, is like an airplane without a wing. Five or six times, when I had fired all my missiles, I might have been able to hit a MiG if I'd had cannon because I was so close, his motion was stopped in my gunsight.

'When we got the General Electric M-61, which fires 6,000 20 mm shells a minute, it turned out to be the greatest gun ever built for a fighter. It jammed very little. One of our rather exceptional pilots, Captain Darrel Simmons, shot down two MiGs with this Gatling gun in one day. He got them where he wanted them and just tapped the trigger twice for a total of 494 rounds. Of my eighteen or more MiG scraps, the longest one was just fourteen minutes. You have only a few seconds to fire in any MiG engagement, so I found our single Gatling's 6,000 rounds per minute more than adequate.

'A trainable gun on a fighter's centreline might be a good idea if it would swivel up and down, as well as sideways, to keep tracking the MiG you're following. It would have to be tied to our lead-computing gunsight, which works beautifully. I should think such a fighter would have to have a rather broad frontal area, which might be a penalty.

'Of course, our missiles are being improved. They ought to be at least as manoeuvrable as the target. If you have to get an enemy to hold still in one little piece of sky so that your missile will do a good job on him, then your missile isn't very good. Regardless of its sophistication, the missile ought to be simple. You've got to be able to maintain it in the dust and downpour, not just on the test range back home. Since you must make lightning-fast decisions in a dogfight, the process of firing missiles must be made less complicated. By the same token any air-to-ground weapons system that requires you to fly in a straight line for more than twenty seconds is no good. Maybe fifteen seconds, but certainly not twenty.

'All future fighters designed to operate in heavily defended areas should have built-in ECM — not for track-breaking, but to jam the SAM's onboard acquisition and guidance radars. If you hang ECM outside the fighter, you have to give up ordnance or fuel. I don't think much of some of the proposals I've heard for an electronic tail watcher to let you know when a MiG is getting on your tail. These devices are based on the assumption that you have the time to sit there and work out an electronic identification programme. They're good for only the last two aircraft in the formation. While you get one MiG, another gets you.

Development of the SUU-16 gun pod made a significant difference to USAF success over North Vietnamese MiGs. Here Airman Second Class David Stopper adjusts the ram-air turbine which rotated the six barrels of the Vulcan gun, at Dan Nang. Prior to firing, the turbine 'fan' swung into the slipstream as shown. *(USAF)*

'Our air-to-air communications, however, certainly warrant improvement — most of it human. We use three frequencies, plus the backseat pilot's intercom. If I see a MiG ten miles out in front of me I want to maintain communications discipline. But in the excitement, it sometimes sounds like the whole strike force grabs the air. It's hard to get a word in edgewise. How to improve this situation never appears on any charts, graphs or curves.

'When I first arrived in Thailand, I heard that some pilots flying F-4s down south wished they could do away with the guy in the back seat and substitute extra fuel. But up in the north, in the enemy's backyard, that won't work. You need the back-seater's extra eyes and total attention for operating your radar system. A one place fighter is fine in your own backyard where our Air Defence Command F-102 interceptor pilots usually operate. In this permissive environment, they can make the interception with that big square building on the ground doing a lot of the radar work for them. If an F-4 driver puts his head down in the cockpit to operate radar during an air-to-air scrap, deep in enemy territory, he's dead.

'Some of our weapons were old-fashioned, but our inertial navigation and radar systems are outstanding. We had an old-fashioned communications control head on the F-4C, but it had none of the maintenance problems of the more easily operated "latest" head on the F-4D. The C had no lead-computing gunsight, which was first installed on the D. We've had humidity and condensation problems you'd never believe, yet maintenance at such bases as Da Nang and Cam Rahn Bay was fantastically good. I'd be proud to have those maintenance people and their equipment back here in the States. While our new equipment is getting increasingly sophisticated, we've got to keep shooting for simpler upkeep and maintenance.

'Perhaps the biggest lesson Clobber College over there taught us is that dogfighting today is surprisingly like our experience in World War 2 and Korea. We found ourselves doing the things that people in the Services swore would never be done again. "Squadron formation, Colonel Olds? You're a romanticist. You're thinking in the past. You have to think in the future. As a matter of fact, you'll never dogfight again. You don't need a gun because you have missiles."

'These predictions and some others proved to be tactically unsound. We and the enemy advance along parallel lines. Basically, little has changed.

'I read a piece in the *Stars and Stripes* attributed to someone in the Department of Defense — this was about mid-1967. In effect the spokesman declared to the world that SAMs didn't bother him because they had shot an awful lot of them and they hadn't hit too many airplanes. All of us were tempted to let him know that, although the MiGs and SAMs didn't scare him, they scared the hell out of us.

'In the final analysis, in addition to the electronics, countermeasures and all the other goodies, it's still a pilot's eyeballs and skill that permit him to operate in that environment of flak, MiGs and SAMs. Even though you may be jamming with some measure of success against the enemy's capabilities to detect you, to launch his missiles and to guide on to you; nevertheless when he launches 38 of them at you in a period of about two minutes, you are compelled to dodge because the odds are against you and Russian Roulette is an idiot's game. I for one, haven't the courage to sit there and watch a missile coming at me, growing larger every instant of time, and say to myself, "That's all right, that electronic gadget down

Robin Olds scored his second MiG kill in *63-7668*. Regular rotation of aircraft usually meant that the aircraft, rather than the pilot was credited with MiG kills. Personal aircraft flown over long periods were rare. *(MacSorley via Pennick)*

under my wing is going to take care of it". No sir. I'm a prudent man. I make a move. We all had to. This is something that you must cope with every instant of time over North Vietnam. It is a test range.

'Speaking of sophisticated equipment and the application of old tactics; you gave us an airplane that will exceed Mach 2 yet with rare exceptions, very few times did we exceed Mach 1 in our strike operations. Instead the power inherent in that capability was translated into an amazing payload at considerable range. The speed potential carried us in swiftly and, once free of our bombs, gave us unbeatable manoeuvring potential. We also fell back on basic and simple tactics — mass flight and element integrity, radio discipline, mutual support, swift action and visual coverage.

'There was a time, not ten years ago, when the suggestion of a need for training in squadron-sized formations, for maintenance of qualification in delivering conventional ordnance and for keeping current in aerial combat tactics, was enough to get one laughed out of the conference room. The name of the game was nuclear deterrence. Everyone, even fighter pilots, worked at it. Over North Vietnam, the MiGs were worrisome. However we liked them because they kept our morale up: All fighter pilots have a love for aerial battle. It's a great feeling to launch a missile at a MiG, even if the missile misses. At least you feel useful. After the mission you can tell terrible war stories about what a scrap you had.

'The power that gives the F-4 the capability to fly Mach 2 translates into a useful load-carrying capacity of two 370 gallon [1,682 litre] tanks, six 750 lb [340 kg] bombs, four Sparrow missiles, two Sidewinder missiles and an ECM pod. Now you don't go Mach 2 with all that under your F-4. So the MiG-17s were a real challenge. They were tough. I've seen a MiG split-S from about 2,000 ft [610 m] going at a great rate of knots. I watched it with amazement. I just couldn't believe it. One of the few times I went supersonic in that whole year occurred when I was firing a Sparrow at a MiG which I thought I had dead to rights. I launched my missile within all parameters and even had time to check my own speed. I was going 1.2 Mach. As the missile accelerated the MiG started turning — made a firing pass on me. I couldn't believe my eyes. I told my back-seater "Look at him! You know what he's going to do? He's going to shoot at us." And he did!

'The MiG-21 has a great "Press". It's a glamorous looking little bird and, if used properly, can be dangerous. But I don't think they ever got the hang of the thing. In spite of all the energy/ manoeuvrability curves and everything I've read in all the books and technical publications, an F-4 can hack a MiG-21 below 15,000 ft [4,572 m] any day. It's not easy! You've got a tremendous fight on your hands. It's kind of discouraging sometimes to run out of missiles. You want to drop your tail hook and try to tear the MiG's canopy off. Basically the '21 was rather a disappointing airplane. It seldom lived up to its press — thank goodness. We had a great respect for the MiG-17s though.

'With rare exception, you didn't have time to use all the sophisticated gear we had in the F-4 when you were over the barrel. Simplicity and speed of execution were paramount. For instance we flew 24 hours round the clock and many of our missions were up in the Delta at night. How did you get in: very simple — headquarters agreed that you should only go in when the moon was at a certain angle and a certain degree of fullness, and you didn't have too many clouds hanging about. Under these conditions, you'd sneak in through the mountains, keeping the front seat completely blacked out. [No lights in the cockpit whatsoever.] The kid in the back seat handled the throttles and watched the compass, and the guy up front flew the bird and served as your terrain avoidance gear.

'You poked your nose over the Delta and got down to about fifty feet [15 m] at 500 knots at night. The land/water contrast of the moon shining on the rice paddies and the canals gave you your horizon. Pretty soon you didn't need that, because the flak started coming up and and you had to be precise — you pulled up to 200 ft [60 m] to drop your bombs when you arrived at the target.

'Equipment sophistication in that environment? You could go in through the same mountains in an advanced airplane using the gear which provides terrain avoidance, but very probably not as low as you could fly if you were doing it for yourself. You'd go in over the Delta at an altitude surely not less than something like 250 ft [76 m]. In the F-4, we pulled up to 200 ft [60 m] to bomb and got right back down again. You say, "What are you idiots doing at fifty feet at night?" Because we all wanted to survive. Because you could not go at 500 or 1,000 ft [50 or 300 m]. Because night time no longer works to your advantage. Night doesn't hide you. It makes it difficult for you; and it doesn't faze the enemy defences.

'When a SAM is launched at you at night you can see it, all right, but you don't know how far away it is. In some instances you can't really tell its relative motion to your position and direction of travel, which is most important in keeping a missile from pelting you. Then when the sustainer motor burns out, the missile doesn't have running lights. It is a very eerie sensation to know that these things are stalking you and you can't see them — except when they burst in a hideous blast of orange flame. I have been chased by SAMs down below 100 ft [30 m] in daylight, so don't tell me they can't track you below certain altitudes. They can.

'So the only way to get in at night is to get down to below fifty feet. That's not a very sophisticated way to do it, but it's the only effective way, and even that is not very safe.

'I tried to remind my troops and those for whom we worked that the China-Burma/India theatre in World War 2 was the place where they invented the Ground Observer Corps. It was the place where they had little people up in the hills who said ''Here come the Japs''. Well it's working in reverse now. I think some of the same spotters are still there. You can have all the radar you like, but those same little guys are still up there on mountain tops, eating their rice and bananas and you can't sneak past them. There is no way. I know, I tried.

'I was once directed [on 30 March 1967] to drop bombs on the blast furnaces at Thai Nguyen in daylight, in bad weather. It was a very fascinating trip. We sneaked in when the visibility was about three-quarters to one mile [1,200-1,600 m] at the most, [and] let down in a part of the map where it says 'relief data inaccurate'. That was very encouraging.

'We were some 1,200 ft [366 m] below the reported tops of the mountains that were all around us before I saw the ground. We immediately had to pull up over a crest, then back down the other side. Anyway, we made it down through the clouds, broke out at 800 feet [244 m] over the Red River. It was on time-and-distance — 3,500 ft [1,067 m] hills half a mile behind us. Three of us proceeded into the target at about twenty ft [6 m]. They didn't start shooting at us until we were about fifteen miles [24 km] out. That's where the first perimeter of guns were. They weren't worried. They knew we were coming, they knew where we were going — they had it all figured out.

'The first two bullet holes through my airplane [we were flying at twenty feet at about 550 knots] were from the top to the bottom. They were shooting from rock hummocks which were all around. It was very difficult, under these particular circumstances, to surprise anybody.

An inspiration to all new crews was the sign above the entrance to the Wolfpack's Ubon flight operations building. A fraction of the Wing's final MiG tally of 38.5 is shown in red stars. *(Pennick)*

American pilots often saw SA-2s in time to evade them. This SAM was intended for an RF-4C which took its picture after launch in 1971. *(USAF)*

'Some interesting things have come out of this war that will write a page in aerial history. There are lessons to be learned but it's going to take a long time to translate this in terms of equipment and men.

'First lesson: the young kids of today. They are better trained than I was; they're smarter; they'd got just as much guts; they're just as patriotic and just as loyal.

'Second lesson: We have to remember that when we are against a very determined enemy, a very capable enemy, a well supplied and well-equipped and courageous enemy, it takes a combination of excellent equipment, fine men and good tactics to do the job.'

# Chapter 10
# Prelude to pullout

The start of 1968 seemed to offer some chance that Ho Chi Minh's regime would be willing to make positive moves towards a ceasefire; overtures made late the previous year were reacted to positively by the US, which had for some time been trying to anticipate the future course of the war. An increasingly attractive option was running down the war effort: having already cost the US taxpayer billions of dollars and many American lives, the war represented an enormous drain on resources — but one which, having come this far, the Americans did not feel they could simply walk away from.

The North Vietnamese had their own plans as the new year began. Hurt by battlefield troop casualties and bombing at home, they devised an operation ostensibly aimed at proving popular support for the communists in selected areas throughout South Vietnam. Taking the form of a military offensive under cover of Tet, the sacred lunar new year holiday, which lasted from 29 to 31 January, the Viet Cong troops who would handle the operation reckoned on a fair degree of surprise, 'pacification' of 36 out of 44 provincial capitals and wholesale popular commitment to the North's cause — a major step towards 'unification' of both areas of the country as one Vietnam.

While the VC planned their coup, the USAF maintained the bombing, alert to any positive move to halt it in the pursuance of peace terms acceptable to its own interests and those of the Saigon government. Slimming down strike forces in order to provide more aircraft for MiGCAP duties and offer the bombers better protection, the Air Force maintained the pressure on lines of communication, concentrations of transportation and industrial areas. January 1968 also recorded a number of MiG interceptions and on the 3rd both sides clashed for the first time in the new year.

Four F-105 strike and two Iron Hand flights bound for the Dong Dau rail bridge in the Hanoi area, were covered by two MiGCAP flights of F-4Ds. Half-heartedly attacked by MiG-21s on approach, Alpha force bored into the attack, no US aircraft being hit. Bravo force was composed entirely of Phantoms — three strike, one flak suppressor and two MiGCAP flights — targeted against the rail yards at Trung Quang. This force was engaged by MiG-17s on withdrawal, the enemy fighters being unable to concentrate their forces as each US element used different timings and routes into their targets, to split the defences.

Both MiG-17s that were shot down fell to 8th TFW crews, the first being destroyed by a strike force F-4D crewed by Lieutenant Colonel Clayton Squier and First Lieutenant Michael Muldoon of the 435 TFS. They engaged four MiG-17s in a head-on pass, having released their ordnance, about six miles (9.5 km) south of Bac Giang. The MiGs passed within 200-300 ft (60-90 m) of the F-4 which chandelled to the left in afterburner to pursue. Muldoon cooled an AIM-4 and after a turn of about 360 degrees, visually acquired two MiGs three miles (5 km) ahead, in trail and making gentle left turns. Selecting the last MiG, Muldoon closed to make positive identification of the aircraft types and launched a Falcon.

Muldoon reported: 'The missile tracked directly to the aft section of the MiG-17 and impacted in a ball of fire and smoke. The MiG immediately started a solid trail of gray/white smoke and continued in a gentle left turn with no manoeuvring observed. As I passed to the right rear of the MiG-17 and slid to the outside of the turn, other aircraft in the immediate area diverted my attention and I lost sight of the smoking aircraft. I gathered my flight together and continued the egress.'

Muldoon's kill was confirmed by other pilots who saw it fall and impact. A second MiG had made a firing pass on Muldoon's aircraft while he was pursuing his quarry, and his wingman was also fired upon by another pair. No damage was sustained by the Phantoms, it being thought that the enemy pilots opened up from too great a range.

One MiGCAP flight saw the action and descended to take a closer look. Major Bernard Bogoslofski and Captain Richard Huskey, flying lead, went after the MiG-17 firing at Muldoon and Squier's wingman. Bogoslofski reported: 'The MiG

Not what it might seem at first glance, this RF-4C carries the name and insignia of the 479th TFS —although there was no copyright on names, particularly if they fitted the role. The RF-4 series gave the US air forces excellent pre-and post-strike target information. *(R. L. Ward)*

An Assam Dragon F-4D (*66-8772*) heads home at low level after a sortie in 1968. *(USAF)*

was tracking one F-4 in a tight left turn and gunfire was observed coming from it. I was high and five o'clock to him and rolled in from 11,000 ft [3,353 m] at an estimated eighty degree dive angle. I tracked the MiG and began firing 20 mm. The MiG tightened his left turn and I performed a vertical pirouette left in order to continue tracking him, using high-G and at least eighty degrees of dive angle, high angle off. A burst of fire appeared on the MiG's left wing and fragmentation of the aircraft's wing was observed as I initiated a recovery.'

Major Albert Borchik in aircraft four of Bogoslofski's flight, and Major Ronald Markey commanding aircraft three, saw the MiG pilot eject. Both these officers also saw it hit and were able to confirm their colleague's kill.

Rolling Thunder continued to exert pressure on the North Vietnamese while final plans were made to carry out the ill-conceived and badly miscalculated Tet offensive as well as what seemed to some as a North Vietnamese attempt to win a Dien Bien Phu-type victory at Khe Sanh. But while the enemy ground forces completed their plans for these two major assaults there was little evidence that a simultaneous effort was to be made by the NVNAF against American air strikes — as might have seemed logical.

Three days before the first NVA artillery shells began falling on Khe Sanh, Major Kenneth Simonet and First Lieutenant Wayne Smith of the 435th TFS added yet another MiG-17 to the mounting tally of aerial kills. Briefed to hit Hai Gia, Dap Cau and the Bac Giang thermal power plant was a three-pronged force: Alpha consisted of an F-4 strike flight supported by Iron Hand, flak suppressor and MiGCAP flights, the latter being at half strength due to two Phantoms having to abort because of ECM malfunctions; Bravo force was four F-105 strike flights plus one Iron Hand flight and an F-4D MiGCAP flight; Charlie force had four 'Thud' strike flights, one of Iron Hand aircraft and two of F-4D MiGCAP — a combined total of 66 aircraft. Only Charlie force, assigned to bomb the Dap Cau railway bypass, escaped unscathed. Alpha and Bravo aircraft were engaged with both MiG-21s and MiG-17s, their attacks sparing the Ha Gia railway sidings from further damage as the 'Thuds' were forced to jettison ordnance two minutes from the target.

Alpha Force also met opposition, from AA and SAMs as well as MiGs. Both lead and number two Phantoms from the strike element were shot down, the lead, crewed by Simonet and Smith, having previously despatched a MiG-17. Eyewitnesses confirmed their single MiG-17 kill.

As Alpha Force approached Bac Giang and initiated a descent from 12,000 ft (3,658 m), aircraft four (Captain Robert Rutherford) saw two MiG-17s at his one and two o'clock sectors, making climbing left turns. Releasing his Walleye air-to-ground missile early, Rutherford executed a hard right climbing turn in company with number three. The flight leader and his wingman made a normal target approach and released their loads before making their own climbing right turn. Two more MiGs had meanwhile appeared, in trail with the first pair.

Aircraft two barely had time to call 'They're shooting' before he was hit. On fire, the F-4D crashed about a mile from the target. No parachutes were seen.

Simonet and Smith, meanwhile, found a third MiG at ten o'clock as they continued upwards in a right turn. Simonet immediately reversed left, cooled an AIM-4D, and fired. An accurate guide was followed by an explosion in the MiG's tailpipe. On fire, the MiG fell away and was seen to crash. But Simonet and Smith were jumped by a fourth MiG and cannon fire raked the Phantom. Trailing smoke, it turned east and withdrew from the battle area, the MiG breaking off the attack. Smoke rapidly turned to raw flame and Simonet and Smith ejected, both 'chutes deploying properly. Post-mission gun camera film analysis and combat reports by other crews confirmed their kill.

No enemy aircraft claims were filed for the rest of January 1968 but on 5 February a MiG-21 fell to a 433rd TFS crew. It was believed at the time that this enemy pilot was acting on his own, without the benefit of GCA control, for he came tearing into a Phantom MiGCAP in a high rear quarter pass. Breaking, the flight of F-4Ds pounced on it. Three crews fired AAMs but missed. Other MiGs appeared on the scene but the one that had made the initial pass ended up in front of the F-4 flown by Captain Robert Boles and First Lieutenant Robert Battista.

Obtaining radar lock-on, Boles requested a clearance to fire from his wingman, Captain Joel Aronoff. Waiting for the return radio call, Boles kept after the MiG which made a series of climb-descend turns. When Aronoff cleared Boles to fire, only one AIM-7 launched but with full system lock-on it guided well and hit the MiG in the aft quarter of the left wing root. Seconds beforehand the MiG rocked its wings left as if the pilot was about to make another turn, or was glancing back to see what his pursuer was doing. He was too late.

On 12 February the Wolfpack covered a strike force bound for Kep airfield but adverse weather conditions forced a diversion to the secondary target, Cao Nung railyard. Both MiGCAP flights watched out for the bombers as they egressed the target and escorted them to the coast. Returning to sweep the target area, the 8th's F-4s were en route out for the second time when both flights tracked a pair of MiG-21s at a point 75 miles (120 km) east of Hanoi.

Flight leader Lieutenant Colonel Alfred Lang, Jr, and First Lieutenant Randy Moss scored the one victory of this mission, setting up the kill in true textbook fashion. Advising his number two that he had a good lock-on at 22 miles (35 km) range, Lang had a running commentary from Moss, his GIB. Passing azimuth, altitude, range and overtake speed to his AC, Moss did not forget the need to check armament switches and fuel state. At eight miles (13 km) range Moss confirmed that the aim dot was centred and that the Phantom was ideally placed for a kill. Moss called ranges at one-mile (1.6 km) intervals until Lang launched two AIM-7E Sparrows at 4½ miles (7 km), visual confirmation that it was a MiG-21 having been made at six miles (9.5 km) range. With full system lock-on, altitude around 34,000 ft (10,360 m) and airspeed at 1.3 Mach, Lang tracked two good shots — the first AIM-7 exploded in the MiG's seven-eight o'clock position and the second in his ten o'clock. Flying through the explosions, the MiG rolled inverted, yawed right to the direction of flight and went into a tumbling spin which quickly became uncontrollable. Lang and Moss then acquired lock-on to a

Fuze adjustments being made to extended nose spike bombs designed to dig into the ground and spread the blast. *(USAF)*

second MiG and closed. But the thirsty J79 engines of the F-4 prevented any further action and the MiGCAP broke off at bingo fuel state.

In confirming the Lang/Moss claim, the 7th Air Force also examined a second by Captain Robert Spencer and First Lieutenant Richard Cahill, his GIB. They felt sure that the MiG flight leader had gone into an uncontrollable spin when their two AIM-7s had exploded in its vicinity — as did other members of the flight. However, this claim was denied.

By this stage of the Rolling Thunder offensive, the USAF was enjoying the fruits of some three years' operational experience, particularly in the early detection of MiG attacks. This remained vitally important and the service rarely let the strike and MiGCAP flights down — indeed, not only could strikes be pre-warned of MiG activity, but also what type of tactics the NVNAF could be expected to employ, based on past performance. Despite this the ratio of losses directly attributable to MiGs (as compared with SAMs, AAA and other causes) was to reach 22 per cent in 1968, far worse than the eight per cent recorded in 1967.

It looked likely, therefore, that another round of 'surgical' strikes on MiG bases, carefully timed to catch the maximum number on the ground, would have to be planned for the immediate future. But the American conduct of the Vietnam war was even then undergoing a drastic rethink. At home audiences across America watched aghast as the newsreels told the story of the Tet offensive. The last straw to many was Viet Cong penetration of the US embassy in Saigon — when their troops were 'winning the war', how, they asked, could the enemy not only get into South Vietnam's capital but actually penetrate the grounds of what should have been a highly secure area?

What American TV audiences did not appreciate (because they were not told by a media service which was itself grossly mis-informed) was that they were seeing not a communist victory but a desperate gamble and the beginnings of a defeat. But the psychological effect of the Tet offensive sowed seeds far stronger than Ho Chi Minh would have believed possible, for they were to blossom into fruits of victory seven years later.

Tet broke the will of Lyndon Johnson to personally continue to run the war as President, at the very time when many people, military and civilian alike, urged him to press the advantages gained when the Tet offensive was broken. It was not to be. In a matter of weeks, Johnson would himself back down and stop the bombing in the only area it could have any effect.

Before then, Rolling Thunder entered its final rounds; the premier MiG-killing wing in Thailand continued its success and scored all four of the last victories of this phase of the war. The last two came on 14 February. Phuc Yen airfield was attacked by one F-4D strike flight, two Iron Hand flights and two MiGCAP flights which were divided into 'fast' and 'slow', the former being armed with AIM-7 and AIM-9 AAMs and the other with AIM-7 and AIM-4 plus SUU-23 gun pods. All MiGCAP crews were briefed to expect the by-now routine MiG-17/MiG-21 mix, the older aircraft flying a low wagon wheel orbit with the MiG-21s maintaining a higher altitude.

MiG warnings proved to be correct and the second F-4 flight turned into two MiG-21s even as the strike force was inbound to the target. To the point of radar lock-on, the F-4s covered the MiGs, but they withdrew and the Phantoms rejoined the strike force near Thud Ridge.

Shadowing the US aircraft the MiG pair attacked one of the trailing Iron Hand 'Thud' flights. They caused no casualties but one F-105 element was forced to return to Korat. As the rest of the strike force proceeded into the target area, four MiG-17s attacked.

The F-4 flight was onto them quickly, picking the MiGs up at eleven o'clock, three miles (5 km) away. Apparently detecting the incoming Phantoms, the MiGs went into a defensive wagon wheel at 8,000 ft (2,438 m) north-east of Phuc Yen. To counter this, the F-4s commenced a spiral climbing pass to gain separation before attacking. Flight leader Lieutenant Colonel Wesley Kimball and his wingman, Major Ray Burgess, flashed through the wheel, Kimball chancing a shot with an AIM-4. Without obtaining a high tone for the Falcon, though, he did not launch. Both Phantoms dived through, pulled up at 7,000 ft (2,133 m) and continued climbing. Number three, crewed by Major Rex Howerton and First Lieutenant Ted Voight II, now charged after one of the MiGs intent on getting on the tail of the first two Phantoms. Howerton rolled in about 2,500 ft (760 m) behind the MiG and fired a Falcon. The missile appeared to guide but to be on the safe side, Howerton used the SUU-23, thinking he might have been too close for an effective AIM-4 kill. Cannon fire struck the MiG which shortly afterwards exploded and began to break up; the Falcon was not seen to impact or destruct. The MiG went down in flames with one wing and the tail unit separated.

Kimball and Burgess now made another pass on another MiG, the Aircraft Commander putting 350 rounds of 20 mm fire in the enemy fighter's direction from 2,000 ft (610 m) distance. No hits were observed and with fuel at bingo state, Kimball and Burgess rejoined their flight to exit the area.

The second MiGCAP flight still had fuel reserves and the lead aircraft got one of these same MiGs: Colonel David Williams, Jr, and First Lieutenant James Feighny had seen Kimball's flight attack. Intending to take one of the trailing MiGs, Williams dived down to around 15,000 ft (4,572 m) going at Mach 1.2. He later reported: 'I asked my rear seat pilot if he was locked on and he replied he was sure but wasn't sure it was the right target, so he asked me to put the pipper on him and he selected gyro out and relocked.'

'I fired one AIM-7E in full system lock-on, interlocks in, in-range light on, at approximately three-quarters of a mile (1,200 m). The missile tracked perfectly and detonated near the left side of the MiG's fuselage. The MiG immediately shed its empennage and burst into a bright orange fire in a flat spin. I immediately yo-yoed high and then rolled over to clear my tail.'

Williams saw, as well as his own MiG, the remains of Howerton's, nose down in a snapping spin, minus its left wing. The tail fluttered down after it and the aircraft was seen to impact in a rice paddy north-east of a large river, followed by the second MiG-17 which also went into a rice paddy close to the foot of Thud Ridge and exploded.

More air strikes followed this last major clash with the MiGs in 1968; on 31 March, President Johnson began to restrict the bombing of North Vietnam prior to a complete cessation later in the year. But although the headline grabbing bombing of North Vietnam was curtailed, there was to be plenty more work for the redoubtable Phantom and its crews in the lengthy period between then and the final end of Rolling Thunder.

# Chapter 11
# Stemming the flow

After the 1968 Tet offensive, the US speeded up the 'Vietnamisation' of the war, began withdrawing ground forces and reduced the tempo of the air offensive against the North. Vast amounts of equipment were passed to South Vietnam so that the fighting could continue. In a conflict that was seemingly insoluble, America's massive military effort in SE Asia had, to all intents and purposes, gone sour under a welter of public protest at home.

In the air, Rolling Thunder gradually petered out. On 1 April all bombing north of the 20th parallel was stopped and on the 3rd, the bomb line was on the 19th parallel, air strikes being restricted to targets in the less strategically important Route Packages I, II and the southernmost third of RP III. This move made nearly all North Vietnam a sanctuary area for the NVNAF MiG force, but did not lead to any great increase in enemy aerial forays into the South. Those fighters which did venture out did so under radio silence without CGI to make single firing passes on US aircraft before retreating North at high speed.

Only on 23 May did a sizeable force of MiGs come south of the bomb line — but US and SVNA defences were well able to cope with this. One MiG-21 was destroyed by a Talos missile.

For the tactical fighter and strike bomber wings in Thailand, the wind-down of the air offensive on North Vietnam saw some shift of emphasis; rotation of squadrons introduced some new aircraft and adaptations of others to fulfil important, if less publicised, combat missions. For the crews there was some relief in not having their work continually under scrutiny by the news media, as they went on with the job of consolidating the South Vietnamese position in the event of a ceasefire and total US withdrawal. The war against North Vietnamese supply routes had continued throughout Rolling Thunder but the US 'de-escalation' policy of 1968 saw units such as the 8th TFW engaged increasingly in a war of attrition against convoys, truck parks and radar sites on an around the clock basis. It was a period when the USAF particularly introduced a number of new weapons programmes which were the result of studies made throughout the war. Invariably developed at enormous cost, it was an effort which only a country with the financial resources of the US could meet. It seemed to show that it took highly sophisticated aircraft and systems to find and destroy a sufficient number of ancient soft skinned vehicles, if these were employed by a nation that was willing to sacrifice almost anything to achieve its aims. Conversely, North

Among the types that came to be part of the 8th TFW during Linebacker I was the AC-130 Hercules gunship. A devastating stream of fire could be delivered by these aircraft which with their cannon armament, were the ultimate in this form of warfare, pioneered by the AC-47 Skytrain back in the mid-1960s. This aircraft bears the tailcode of the 16th SOS, attached to the Wolfpack when this photo was taken on 11 June 1972. *(USAF)*

Vietnam had the one resource to make its own proportionately gigantic effort possible in the face of otherwise crippling losses — manpower.

In May 1968, Ubon welcomed three AC-130A Spectre gunships belonging to the 16th Special Operations Squadron. Very heavily armed, these Hercules transport adaptations came under the jurisdiction of the 8th TFW and often flew in company with its F-4s which acted as escorts to suppress flak and added their weight to destroy targets. All such missions were undertaken during the hours of darkness, the AC-130s remaining on station for about three hours. There were usually three Phantoms to cover one gunship.

The premier F-4 night fighter unit was the 8th Wing's 497th TFS, the appropriately named 'Night Owls'. While not alone in launching night Phantom sorties, the Owls were the only squadron in SE Asia solely dedicated to the night missions, flown by the most highly qualified and experienced crews on one of the most demanding assignments of all. It took skill, a cool head and not insubstantial courage to fly a high speed jet fighter over jungle terrain at night, ready when the call came to plunge into a black void to deliver ordnance on a pin-point target. And crews had to master the technique of night refuelling, be adept at accurate navigation, able to hit targets under Loran guidance and, if necessary, visually. These nocturnal tactics were very hard for the enemy to master — or to hide from, as widespread use of infra-red sensors and flares literally turned night into day for the prowling aircrews.

Gunships particularly proved their worth. Able to orbit known transport routes and assembly points along the myriad branches of the Trail, they could await the arrival of 'Charlie' in relative safety, knowing that there was invariably a Phantom about to deal with the defences.

The technique was to have an F-4 arrive in the designated target area just after the AC-130 had reached it. The second Phantom would then launch, rendezvous with a Young Tiger tanker and time his arrival at the target area just as the first fighter had reached bingo fuel state. Relieved on station by number two, the first aircraft would seek a tanker and return to the gunship's beat. A third Phantom would then take off for the area being patrolled and take his turn in the escort relay, each one of the trio flying two escort periods.

Typical ordnance for a Night Owl mission was fragmentation, cluster bombs and napalm. All aircraft would also carry drop tanks as standard, either 370 gallon (1,682 litre) under the wings or a 600-gallon (2,728 litre) on the belly centre line.

When the weather allowed, the gunship/F-4 hunter-killer teams achieved success and undoubtedly disrupted the flow of supplies, men and matériel into

The very high (some would say notoriously so) sortie rate against the North brought records such as this in a remarkably short space of time. At left Capts Tom Walsh and John Brown have 200 missions each, while Maj Bill Henderson, Capt Jimmy Yoshinaka and 1/Lts Ron Morrow, Terry Dielman, Bill Kopcho and Allen Earls have 100 apiece. Completion of the 100 sorties entitled a man to go home — but many volunteered for a second or third tour, particularly with a crack unit like the 497th. *(USAF)*

When the 8th Wing absorbed squadrons after the end of Rolling Thunder, aircraft such as the AC-130 were in effect, fighters . . . this Hercules was one of the early modifications to gunship configuration.

To achieve success against small targets, AC-130s carried a vast array of firepower, including 20-and 40 mm cannon and 7.62 mm miniguns. The 16th Special Operations Squadron flew armed Hercs with the 8th Wing, well protected by Phantoms during their noctural forays. *(USAF)*

Mainstay of the TAC strike effort were Young Tiger KC-135s, represented here by *58-130*, an A model. *(Boeing)*

the South. The flood occasionally was slowed to a trickle, but it was never halted, despite a multi-million dollar effort to dam the road trails.

The Night Owls ably assisted the US interdiction missions by providing fast Forward Air Control (FAC) flights. Flown by night as well as day, the F-4 proved ideal in the face of determined anti-aircraft defences, which were beginning to take a toll of the slower, lightly armed forward air control aircraft assigned to this very important duty. In 1967 F-100s became the first jet FACs under the code name Misty and by the following year, the Phantom had taken over. All fighter Wings seeing service in South-East Asia were subject to changes in squadron composition as units rotated in and out of the theatre on temporary duty assignment. It usually happened that the Wing retained two or three regular squadrons, with two or more joining these at different times. Until the end of Rolling Thunder, the type of aircraft flown and the number maintained remained more or less consistent; it was when the large scale air strikes on the North were terminated that the fighter Wings were slimmed down or composed of squadrons flying a wide variety of different aircraft, carrying out a diversity of specialised tasks.

The Wolfpack continued to fly the F-4C and 'D until the US withdrawal, although the F-4E was to see action before the end. One of the Phantom squadrons to join it after Rolling Thunder had passed its zenith, was the 25th Tactical Fighter Squadron.

On 28 May 1968, twenty F-4Ds of the 25th departed Eglin AFB bound for Ubon. They flew non-stop to Hawaii and employed in-flight refuelling to reach Andersen AB, Guam. Following a short stayover the Phantoms departed for Thailand, their arrival being awaited by the previously positioned maintenance and support echelons, which had been flown in by C-141s. As had become standard procedure, the 25th's own personnel were supported by smaller mobile teams composed of both military and civilian specialists. The 25th TFS joined the 8th Wing's 433rd, 435th, and 497th squadrons at Ubon and underwent a week's theatre indoctrination training at PACAF's jungle survival school at Clark AB in the Philippines. These courses initiated new crews into SE Asian conditions with emphasis on search and rescue procedures, escape and evasion and combat tactics and techniques employed by the 8th Wing. These lectures, backed up by others at Ubon, gave the newcomers the latest tactical situation and an idea of what to expect when they flew combat missions.

On their first fifteen missions, each 25th TFS crew flew as wingmen to an experienced crew from one of the other squadrons, the flights being led by one of the 'old hands'. By July the 25th was fully self-sufficient and all subsequent missions were led by squadron aircrews.

Although flying missions as an integral part of the Wolfpack, the 25th's role was a little broader in that it was tasked to feed back all details of SE Asian conditions so that the Air Force could add to its knowledge, both of the tactical situation in general and, more specifically, how the F-4 stood up to combat, This stemmed from the 25th's previous assignment at Eglin, where it had been activated on 20 June 1965 as part of the 33rd TFW. The squadron's task was to explore the Phantom's capability, by flying it 'to the limit' in every role it had been

The bases in Thailand and South Vietnam saw thousands of visiting aircraft movements in a short period of time. This F-4D, *66-7646* 'The Toot' belonged to the commander of the 389th TFS, 366th TFW. Applying the name on a 'flag' on the nose was common in this wing, the flag, drop tank tips, canopy trim and fuselage band being red bordered in white. Rudder stripes were red, white and blue. The Gunfighters badge appears on the air intake trunking. *(Via R. L. Ward)*

What the well dressed Phantom driver wore for missions from Thailand circa 1968. The red and white trim around intake and canopy was widely applied to 25th TFS aircraft.

*(F. E. Brandon via R. L. Ward)*

designed to undertake under the Air Force training programme. All aircrews were required to complete this syllabus before being declared as combat ready,

The following mission profiles were flown: intercept training under GCI control; high altitude (targets above 35,000 ft/10,668 m) and low altitude (targets below 3,000 ft/914 m) intercepts; ECM training; attack conversions; snap-up attacks; air combat manoeuvres (day fighter tactics and fighter vs fighter, in flights of two and four); nuclear and conventional weapons delivery, including dive toss bombing, skip bombing, strafing, rocketry and level radar bombing; aerial refuelling; and low-level navigation and ground attack, with or without the aid of forward air control.

In addition, all F-4 aircrews received ground instruction which included proficiency with the .38 pistol and M-16 rifle, a three-week stint at Stead AFB on the USAF survival course and a one-week TAC survival course at Langley. Selected pilots took Forward Air Controller training while others became specialists in weapons, electronic warfare techniques and survival.

During the summer and autumn of 1965, the 25th TFS flew air-to-ground gunnery training courses at Eglin, and air-to-air missions over the Gulf of Mexico.

On 1 November the squadron became the first in the 33rd Tactical Fighter Wing to complete a TAC Operational Readiness Test with the F-4 and was certified combat ready.

Commanded by Lieutenant Colonel Russell E. Taliaferro during its initial Phantom period, the 25th was taken over by Lieutenant Colonel Ethan A Grant on 10 February 1966. Intensive flying training continued. A typical gunnery training sortie had four F-4Cs armed variously with a practice bomb dispenser, gun pod and rocket launchers with three 2.75 in (70 mm) rockets fitted with inert heads. After formation take-off, the flight would adopt tactical formation on a 300-mile (480 km) low-level navigation route at a height of 500 ft (150 m). Approaching the gunnery range, each F-4 crew would space out for individual delivery of practice bombs. When the bomb run had been completed and the scores marked, the flight would rejoin over the range to carry out skip and dive bomb and strafing attacks, before returning to Eglin. Average mission time would be about an hour and a half.

Weapons delivery sorties were flown at speeds varying from 400 to 525 knots with release altitudes varying from 50 ft (15 m) for skip bombing to 2,500-5,000 ft (760-1,524 m) for dive bombing and rocketry. Dive angles were up to ten degrees for skip bombing and between 30 and 45 for dive bombing and rocket attack.

Attacks using live ordnance began early in 1966. Air-to-air launches were made against towed targets using both Sparrows and Sidewinders, and the 2,000 lb (907 kg) BDU-8 bomb with retarding parachute, which was delivered 'under realistic

Almost factory fresh this 25th TFS F-4D *66-8782* also has nose and tail electro-luminescent strips to aid formation-keeping under low light conditions. *(J. W. Boyce via R. L. Ward)*

Even loaded down with strike cameras, a variety of ordnance and fuel tanks, the F-4's good power to weight ratio improved strike requirements out of all proportion compared with other aircraft in the theatre. These 8th Wing F-4Ds were photographed on a mission in November 1971, the 25th TFS machine sporting a black and yellow-checked fin cap. *(USAF)*

conditions'. Sorties were also flown in conjunction with the US Army's Infantry School and the USAF Air Ground Operations School. This two-year phase of training took in firepower demonstrations to show the Army how effective the F-4 could be in the close support role. Exercise Blue Chip, held at Fort Bragg, North Carolina, in April 1966, was impressive. The 25th brought its aircraft in from Myrtle Beach and Seymour Johnson AFBs and put in a week's practice before the start of the demonstration at the Army's own close support school. It was a time when the helicopter versus fixed-wing for Army support controversy was at its height and the Air Force was keen to show that an aircraft such as the Phantom was more than capable of handling any support situation the Army might require. The Army in its turn believed that its own fixed- wing air support would be useful.

Pulling out all the stops during the demonstration, the 25th TFS made a good case for the fixed-wing lobby (USAF branch). The F-4s screamed across the ranges at Mach 1.2, maintaining minimum altitude and releasing a range of ordnance designed to devastate ground targets. The programme included two F-4s in formation, dropping eleven BLU-1 napalm bombs, and loft-bombing with 24 500 lb (227 kg) bombs each; single ship strafing with three gun pods, and firing fifteen-round rocket launchers, thus putting 285 2.75 in (70 mm) rockets on the target, and low altitude drop of BDU-8 dummy bombs. As well as fast delivery, the F-4s flew at 140 knots, almost the minimum for safety.

The 25th began in the spring of 1966 to ferry F-4Cs to South-East Asia and also began to provide replacement aircrews. These flights, under the codename Town

Car, were to take place until mid-1968, when the 25th began its own tour of duty in Thailand. They staged from Eglin to California, without incident, en route flight refuelling being completed successfully. Later in 1966, the 25th picked up new F-4Ds at St Louis and flew these to Asia and the UK.

Re-equipped with the F-4D, the 25th continued its programme of training and equipment-compatibility trials, under the direction of the Tactical Air Warfare Center (TAWC), at Eglin. Sparrow Shoot was the large scale firing of the AIM-7 using an F-101B trailing a five-mile long cable and target. Flying at 35,000 ft (10,668 m), the Voodoo would be 'attacked' by successive waves of F-4s launching missiles from head on and slightly below the target.

Project Dancing Falcon was the programme aimed at marrying the AIM-4 to the F-4D; initially 'captive shoots' were made with inert Falcons, the F-4s testing the reaction of the weapon's infra-red seeker head from lock-ons obtained from other F-4s, F-104s and T-33s flying as targets. Live firings were then made against flares which provided the necessary infra-red heat source. Ryan Firebee drones were next introduced, the first direct hit being made on 15 November 1966. Martin Mace air-breathing missiles were introduced into the Falcon programme from 20

A pair of 8th Wing F-4Ds with laser-guided bombs en route to a target. The laser guidance required some bomb modification, including larger fins for a better 'flight' profile, and the laser seeker head. The nearest aircraft also has the 'towel rack' fuselage aerials for Loran equipment. *(USAF)*

CO of the 25th TFS was Capt Albert Piccirillo, taxiing out in Flave, his F-4D *66-8782*, in November 1968. The aircraft is armed with 750lb bombs fitted with fuze extenders for maximum shrapnel effect, and a strike camera occupies a forward Sparrow missile bay. Above the groundcrew placard is the squadron's Assam Dragon insignia, a carry-over from WW 2. *(Via R. L. Ward)*

December 1966, and this proved to be a more realistic target, mainly because it was similar in size to a fighter aircraft.

Supersonic AIM-4 launches were made against targets provided by the Air Proving Ground Center at Eglin. The attacking F-4 achieved Mach 1.4 at 40,000 ft (12,192 m) and launched in a 4G turn. Launches were made at speeds up to Mach 1.7 and at the conclusion of Dancing Falcon, two drones had been lost, one from being struck by a missile and one through loss of control. The programme seemed to prove that the Falcon had some advantages over the AIM-9 and AIM-7 — but combat would determine the final outcome.

The 25th passed onto Tropic Moon, a test of the F-4D's bombing computer system. Flown throughout the summer of 1967, these tests were all undertaken at night and were used to also evaluate the effectiveness of all-weather attack systems and tactics. Loran-D was also checked out during this phase.

So diverse were the tasks that were being and would in future be assigned to the F-4, that the USAF decided to release the 25th TFS for combat duty and activate a dedicated test and evaluation squadron, the 4533rd Tactical Test Squadron, to replace it at Eglin. It was undoubtedly felt that with the Rolling

Thunder campaign running down, the 25th could continue to supply valuable feedback on a variety of missions in a 'real war' situation.

Alerted for duty in Asia (for the third time in its long history), the 25th completed its combat training phase on 1 May 1968. In command was Lieutenant Colonel Lloyd C. Ulrich. Paintwork began to reflect the unit's World War 2 associations with Asia as each Phantom in the squadron would subsequently receive a large yellow dragon, perpetuating the "Assam Dragons" of two decades previously.

Although the programme to find a more modern Wild Weasel SAM- suppression platform than the F-105 did reach operational status in 1969 with the deployment of the first Weasel F-4Ds to Okinawa, the venerable Thud remained the most important anti-missile aircraft of the Vietnam war. This F-105F *(62-4434)* was the first to be converted to full G model configuration with QRC-380 ECM blisters on the fuselage sides. AGM-78B Standard ARM and AGM-45 Shrike missiles are carried on the wing pylons. (USAF).

# Chapter 12
# Pyrrhic victory

Moves by the North Vietnamese to at least meet with US representatives in Paris to talk peace had the required effect. The Johnson administration, beleaguered by a groundswell of anti-war sentiment at home, acted. On 31 October 1968, Lyndon Johnson announced the end of all air, naval and artillery bombardment of North Vietnam, effective 08.00 hours, Washington time on 1 November.

Ninety minutes before the President spoke, Major Frank C. Lenahan made the last Rolling Thunder target run in an 8th TFW F-4D against an installation near Dong Hoi. On his arrival back at Ubon the most controversial aerial bombing campaign in history came to an end, three years and nine months after it had begun. Tactical Air Command aircraft had logged no less than 304,000 sorties to bring the enemy to the conference table. More bombs had been dropped than in any comparable conflict, on targets which, while important to the enemy, were in no way irreplaceable. During Rolling Thunder there had been little need for tactical aircraft based in Thailand to expend a great part of their time supporting the fighting in South Vietnam. There had been more than enough US and South Vietnamese squadrons available for 'in-country' air strikes. But with impending US troop withdrawals and a rapid build-up of SVNAF strength the TAC squadrons in Thailand embarked on an intensive period of flying equally as demanding as the strikes on the North had been. The USAF also became the prime military arm to support Vietnamisation 'in the field' and although squadrons did leave the theatre, the peace talks only slowed the pace. Neither did the war against the North cease entirely. Under the terms of the truce the US obtained sanctions to continue reconnaissance flights north of the DMZ, rightly assuming that the bombing would usher in a feverish North Vietnamese effort to repair damaged facilities, re-open communications and rebuild anti-aircraft defences.

With Richard Nixon in the White House there followed a period of tough talking and frequent shows of strength to prove that the US had by no means abandoned South Vietnam to a possible takeover by the North. When the US reconnnaissance flights began to be fired upon, TAC sent fighter-bombers to protect them, and also mounted raids in direct retaliation to the previously-agreed immunity being ignored.

Ample evidence was forthcoming from photo sorties to show that the North was indeed using the breathing space profitably. It became a well known fact that

Bright red trim was applied to 'Ol' Eagle Eye, alias F-4D *66-7764* of the 433rd at Ubon in November 1968. *(Via R. L. Ward)*

Close up of the nose of *66-7764* showing salient details, including the squadron 'badge', and nickname painted under both canopies on the starboard side. *(Via R. L. Ward)*

This 25th TFS F-4D carries MK-82 bombs with fuze extenders on a sortie out of Ubon on 30 January 1970. *(USAF)*

the enemy was a master of 'make do and mend' and in the months after Rolling Thunder, his enormous workforce rapidly restored the country back to more or less working order, or so it seemed. There was certainly no lack of new military equipment in the country — the writing was very much on the wall.

'Protective reaction' (PR) and 'reinforced protective reaction' (RPR) strikes against Northern targets may have shown the enemy that, while the US had abandoned the mass bombing raids of previous years, its potency had proportionately increased. Fewer aircraft using laser-guided munitions or 'smart' bombs as they became widely known were able to achieve far higher degrees of damage than before. RPR strikes were directed against the North Vietnamese air defence systems beginning on 1 May 1970. Air Force and Navy aircraft combined as a 500-plus force to hit SAM and AAA sites and NVA logistic facilities around the Barthelemy Pass, Ben Karai Pass and sectors immediately north of the DMZ. In a four-day period, these attacks destroyed or disabled most of these sites, which were located nearer the South than ever before. By November the greater part of the 48,064 sorties by USAF aircraft in 1970 had been flown.

By that time the USAF fighter squadrons in Vietnam and Thailand were predominantly equipped with the F-4. The 8th TFW remained at Ubon with F-4Ds; the 388th had two squadrons of F-4Es at Korat and the 432nd Tactical

Reconnaissance Wing was at Udorn with four squadrons of F-4Ds. In addition there were three Phantom wings in South Vietnam plus squadrons equipped with a diversity of types ranging from AC-130 Hercules gunships, B-57s to F-105s, which continued to fly both tactical fighter sorties and perform the Wild Weasel missions pending further development work on the Weasel F-4D.

Vietnam had long been off the front pages of the world's press, although the fighting continued as the terrible decade of the 1960s slipped into history. The war which already generated dozens of buzz words, phrases and colourful jargon, added before the end of 1971, Lam Son 719, Louisville Slugger and Fracture Cross Alpha. Not so new, were Igloo White and Commando Hunt, the respective 'seeding' of the country in the vicinity of the DMZ to detect the movement of nearby vehicles or people, and the aerial interdiction of Trail routes through Laos. TAC sortie rates began to rise again.

As the 8th Wing turned increasingly to round the clock interdiction, with targets including lines of communication (LOCs), road and river transport and storage areas, so the industrial effort to give operational units new and better weapons began to work through. By far the biggest innovation was the development of laser-guidance for the humble 'iron bomb'. In the autumn of 1968 the 497th TFS had begun training with LGM — Laser Guided Munitions — in order to determine their accuracy and the best attack profiles to be flown. This

Aerial view of the F-4 revetment area at Ubon Royal Thai Air Force Base, on 30 January 1969. *(USAF)*

Close-up view of a camouflaged Phase I ADSID (Air Delivered Seismic Intrusion Device) sensor planted in the ground. Under the Igloo White programme, areas of enemy infiltration were seeded to detect and transmit movement of men and vehicles to a central command post for subsequent air attack. F-4s were among the aircraft that dropped the sensors from special dispensers. *(USAF)*

project was transferred to the 433rd TFS and on 24 October, a 'Satan's Angels' flight dropped the first of the new weapons. Loran D navigation had also been used by the other squadrons for some time, and the 433rd received its first Phantoms so equipped early in 1969. An all weather system, Loran-D was much more versatile and accurate than radar bombing. Combined with LGMs it gave the Thailand-based F-4 squadrons unrivalled versatility, enabling good bombing results to be achieved under almost any conditions.

The so-called 'smart bombs' which made such a difference to US pilots' ability to disable and destroy targets which had withstood countless tons of conventional ordnance for years, came in two types: EOGBs — Electro-Optical Guided Bombs and Laser Guided Bombs — LGBs. The EOGB was a 2,000 lb (907 kg) bomb with a small TV camera attached to the nose which transmitted a picture of what it was seeing to a screen in the aircraft. The pilot would simply point his aircraft and EOGB at the target to allow the WSO to acquire it on his 'scope, refine the contrast aiming point and designate the target to the weapon. Once this was done, the pilot released and departed the target area, leaving the EOGB to guide itself onto the designated aiming point. A successful hit was reliant on good visibility but if this was available the EOGB invariably impacted on the aiming point.

In the LGB a laser sensor mated to the nose of a 2,000 or 3,000 lb (907-1,360 kg) bomb would guide on a target 'illuminated' with low power laser energy generated by a designator pod carried by the attacking fighter. The pod contained

After Rolling Thunder the Night Owls went increasingly over to nocturnal sorties — hence the black lower surface paint seen here on F-4D *66-7457* in December 1968 when Maj Bill Campbell was the AC. *(Via R. L. Ward)*

F-4Ds *60-234* of the 435th TFS and *65-705* of the 433rd lead other Wolfpack Phantoms on an LGB sortie in 1972. *(USAF)*

an optical viewing system and laser emitting capability, both operated by the WSO, who optically located the target aiming point and used the laser to illuminate it.

Again the pilot would release the bomb and leave the target area, the LGB continuing to home onto the aiming point down the laser 'cone' or 'basket' created by the pod. One disadvantage was that the target had to be continuously illuminated by the laser for the LGB to be guided accurately; if cloud obscured the view, the smart bomb would not guide and would probably miss. On the other hand, more than one aircraft at a time could attack with LGBs, all weapons using the same illumination point to guide on. As the 8th Wing became proficient in the use of LGBs the crews realised that there had been many targets in North Vietnam that were tailor-made for such weapons — particularly the notorious Paul Doumier and Thanh Hoa bridges — but at present these were once again 'off limits'.

On 21 September 1971 the USAF struck the Dong Hoi area with 196 aircraft, heavily damaging POL facilities. MiG bases were attacked again on 7-8 November and the first USAF 'force enhancement' units began to arrive in Vietnam and Thailand in response to a steady increase in NVA activity north of the DMZ. Something was definitely brewing.

By December the Air Force had 277 aircraft stationed in South Vietnam — a small number compared with a June 1968 high of 737 but the figure was rising. Early in 1972 numerous sorties were mounted against stockpiled enemy supplies in sanctuary areas north of the DMZ. March saw TAC step up sorties to an average 15,000; the last Commando Hunt series of strikes end and the Paris peace talks making the by-now routine lack of progress. The North Vietnamese needed a few more weeks . . .

Richard Nixon's pledge to aid South Vietnam in the event of any serious threat held good — and history seemed to be repeating itself as the base photo labs developed ample evidence of a regenerated North Vietnamese Air Force. By late 1971 it was reliably estimated that the enemy had around 250 MiGs on hand, ninety of them MiG-21s. Part of the force had already ventured across the border and MiGs had been encountered over Laos. Among the aircraft that returned to SE Asia at that time were EC-121 Constellations, needed to resume their radar watch on MiG activity.

As Johnson had before him, Nixon fervently hoped for a solution to the war without having to unleash US airpower in a way that his Democratic forebear had been unwilling to do. After Christmas 1971, the USAF launched a five-day series of strikes which were the largest in terms of sorties — 1,025 — since Rolling Thunder. This and subsequent operations were firm enough reminders (as if these were necessary) of US might in the air.

North Vietnam made its long-awaited move on 29 March. Having amassed some 200,000 men the NVA crashed into Military Region I, directly south of the DMZ, and simultaneously penetrated into MR II through Laos. It was an unprecedented show of force on the part of the NVA, a conventional style land invasion with infantry supported by tanks and AFVs, very different to the guerrilla style of war that had been fought before. Given US and SVNAF air superiority it was unlikely to achieve much without cripplingly high casualties

Armed to the teeth Owl F-4D *66-7468* taxiing out of the Ubon arming area in late 1968. *(Via R. L. Ward)*

F-4D *60-234* of the 435th TFS configured with two LGBs, AIM-7s, drop tanks and an ECM pod. The red tail tip, as well as the tail code, served to identify the squadron. *(USAF)*

but for some days aircraft were forced to ride out a period of inclement weather which kept them on the ground.

Through early April 1972 the North Vietnamese consolidated the gains they had made largely unhampered by air attack. They were up against untested South Vietnamese troops in the DMZ region and achieved enough surprise to carry them forward to Dak To, occupy ridge positions west of Kontum and threaten Pleiku. Artillery shelled Dak To airfield and curtailed air operations.

Defending forces were surprised not only by the enemy's numerical superiority, but by new weapons such as T-54 tanks and SA-7 anti-tank and AT-13 wire guided missiles and 130 mm guns. These and older Soviet-made tanks and guns were able by mid-month to establish a bridgehead and the enemy fed in 20,000 more troops to assist those who had originally crossed the border.

They thrust into Military Regions I, II and III, the latter being the most serious as the communist objective was to neutralise the towns and airfields at Loc Ninh, An Loc and Quan Loi and cut highway 13 which connected Binh Long province with Saigon. The advance continued, under the assumption that the US would

Highly successful when laser guided weapons could not 'see' the target was the EOGB, seen here on the inboard racks of two F-4s. *(Via R. L. Ward; USAF)*

not risk committing its airpower to another bout of combat. The North Vietnamese gambled that Nixon would be subject to the same pressures as Johnson had been and would stay his hand in the face of the anti-war sentiment at home. This confidence was misplaced.

When the weather improved, American and South Vietnamese pilots went after a plethora of targets more or less over open sites. Rarely before had the enemy presented himself like this and concentrated his forces so that, despite a formidable array of AAA weapons, his men, vehicles and supplies were very vulnerable to attack from the air. The Americans and South Vietnamese made the most of the opportunity. It was unfortunate for the North that the incumbent US President was determined to finish his country's involvement in the war by wresting as much as he could from an unenviable situation. And at that point his

Another SAM on its way to take out a USAF RF-4C during the latter's photo run over the Red River area in 1971. *(USAF)*

Along with the stateside support squadrons that brought the F-4E to SE Asia, the in-theatre 388th TFW relinquished the trusty Thud and converted to this model in November 1968, the first SE Asian wing to do so. This aircraft, *67-230* 'Can-Do' hailed from the 34th TFS.
*(J. W. Boyce via R. L. Ward)*

armed forces had finally been equipped with weapons that could exact a terrible toll if he had the will to turn them loose, free of any restrictions on where and what they should attack.

Nixon himself, taking something of a gamble in that there was a possibility if the US reacted strongly, that the impending summit talks would be cancelled by the Russians, decided that the country would prefer losing at the super powers' conference table to abandoning South Vietnam to its fate at that stage. Linebacker was given the go-ahead. In a 'go for broke' mood, Nixon ordered an all-out effort by US airpower to rout the North Vietnamese offensive and show Hanoi that he wanted a return to the Paris peace talks — and quickly. If that could be achieved only at the expense of more Vietnamese targets, so be it.

Linebacker operations started with Pocket Money, the Navy's aerial mining campaign against North Vietnamese ports, particularly Haiphong. Sown on 9 May, the mines were set to activate at 18.00 hours on 11 May, giving the 35 foreign ships then in port ample time to leave.

Air Force and Navy land targets included the road links with China, the main railways and bridges in North Vietnam, and the stockpiled military hardware that had been flowing into the country for years. There were still some areas denied to US airmen, including the Hanoi thermal power plant, the international radio centre, the party headquarters and Gia Lam airport. The availability of EOGB and LGB weapons meant that military targets could be hit with far more precision than hitherto when Rolling Thunder guidelines precluded numerous targets due to their proximity to civilian dwellings.

As of 31 March the USAF had 95 F-4s at Da Nang and Korat, plus 52 at Udorn; the 8th TFW had seventy Phantoms at Ubon along with ten B-57s and thirteen AC-130s. This formidable force was boosted as Constant Guard I deployments were made from the US. Among these were two F-4 squadrons (the 334th and 336th) of the 4th Fighter Wing, destined for duty at Ubon and Udorn respectively.

On 8 April the 334th's eighteen F-4Es left Seymour Johnson AFB, North Carolina, and headed for Hickam, Guam and Ubon, where they arrived on the 11th. The following day another eighteen aircraft arrived in good order, to fly their first combat sorties on the 14th. Constant Guard I and II brought another 36 F-4Es into the war zone, TAC commanders thus achieving some assurance that if another bout of air combat with the NVNAF should ensue, Phantom crews would have the advantage of a built in gun. The F-4E also had updated radar and a generally improved performance over the F-4D, which remained the most numerous variant operated by the SE Asian-based wings. Capable, as were most variants, of hauling a bomb load equal to that of the F-4D, the E model became the most versatile of the line.

Further F-4Ds were also flown across the Pacific under Constant Guard III, this deployment using a new system whereby KC-135 tankers accompanied the F-4s all the way instead of meeting them at pre-arranged rendezvous points at roughly 800 mile (1,290 km) intervals. The units moved into Takhli found primitive conditions as the base had been closed in 1971 and placed on a caretaker basis under the Royal Thai Air Force.

The rapid overseas movement of USAF squadrons, of which there were eleven between 8 February and 13 May, also served to show that such short-notice deployments were feasible. On 30 May the newcomers had raised Ubon's total F-4 complement to 92, there being 284 Phantoms in Thailand, with a further 64 at Da Nang and Nakom Phanom. TAC's primary strike force was further boosted by 31 F-105s at Korat.

Towards the end of the war, the 8th TFW diversified and encompassed aircraft other than Phantoms. The B-57 was one of the longest-serving USAF aircraft of the war and conducted many of the early strike sorties before switching to night interdiction. (MAP)

F-4D of the 433rd TFS carrying a mixed load of LGBs and 'iron' bombs for a Linebacker I mission. Note the squadron badge on the air intakes. *(USAF)*

Towards the end of the Vietnam war, reorganisation and rotation home of combat squadrons saw units like the 555th TFS under the jurisdiction of different wing HQs. This F-4D *66-8743* was flying as part of the 432nd TRW circa 1972, the 555th going on to score the highest number of MiG kills by one squadron, 39. *(USAF)*

# Chapter 13
# Bridge busters

Having built its reputation by its prowess in aerial combat, the 'MiG Killer' Wolfpack rapidly took on a new title during Linebacker I — that of 'Bridge Busters'. North Vietnam's bridges had been among the toughest targets of all during Rolling Thunder. Traditionally difficult to destroy by air attack in World War 2 and Korea, bridges were heavily defended, none more so than those in Vietnam. Equipped with smart bombs, the 8th TFW undertook to neutralise the key points of the supply routes, most of which were carrying traffic by the time of the 1972 spring invasion. The enemy had used many ingenious ways of keeping war supplies moving and ferries were widely employed when US air strikes removed one or more sections of bridges in successive raids. Large enough to carry locomotives, these ferries, while slow, enabled the rivers to be crossed. Use was also made of pontoon bridges to span waterways a short distance from the more permanent structures, while these were under repair.

Given a period of bad weather when the American aircraft did not appear, the construction gangs slaved to repair the damage. When bridges were damaged or knocked down again, the process of repair and bypassing began afresh — and was repeated as many times as necessary. Given a long period when repair work was not interrupted by air attack, the North Vietnamese not only effected completion of construction work, but were able to strengthen the most important bridges so that they might withstand any future assault. Of the five most important bridges, the Paul Doumier and Thanh Hoa spans had been subject to particularly heavy air attack during Rolling Thunder. The Paul Doumier was the longest in North Vietnam, carrying a single rail track between flanking roadways across the Red River flood plains on the outskirts of Hanoi. Further south the bridge at Thanh Hoa, known as the Ham Rung or 'Dragon's Jaw', spanned the Song Ma river. Although smaller, the Dragon's Jaw was an important link in the rail network and had previously defied all attempts to destroy it.

On 27 April 1972 the 8th TFW sent out just eight F-4s armed with 2,000 lb (907 kg) LGBs to knock down the Thanh Hoa bridge. Earlier strikes had required scores of F-105s with their impressive — but largely ineffectual in terms of lasting damage — loads of iron bombs. Supporting the eight strike Phantoms launching from Ubon were four F-4 chaff bombers which would lay down a corridor of radar blinding metallic strips to throw off the defending AAA. Taking on fuel en route, the force proceeded north. Bad weather had forced postponement of the strike on previous days and now approaching pilots saw that as well as a protective chaff corridor, they had plenty of cloud cover — but laser guided bombs required clear conditions for a successful laser illumination. Fortunately some of the Phantoms carried EOGBs and these aircraft positioned for an attack, and launched five bombs.

The defences reacted with typical ferocity, even to the extent of firing SAMs as well as thousands of rounds of anti-aircraft shells. But the chaff had done its work well — the F-4s all escaped unscathed. Their bombs had definitely weakened the bridge to the extent that vehicular traffic had to find another way across. Post-mission reconnaissance revealed obvious shock wave damage which had shaken the Dragon to its foundations. Even though it was 'out' for the time being, its reputation as one of the toughest targets in North Vietnam was still intact.

The Wolfpack went after the Paul Doumier bridge on 10 May, combining an LGB strike with an attack on the Yen Bien rail yards. This time the force was much larger, reminiscent of the old days. By coincidence, Captain Thomas 'Mike' Messett, who had flown the August '67 first strike against the bridge, led a two-ship element of an 8th TFW force that comprised 24 aircraft, sixteen carrying LGBs and eight being chaff bombers.

Accompanied by fifteen F-105G Wild Weasel aircraft from the 388th at Korat and four EB-66s for ECM support, plus a MiGCAP of F-4s, the Wolfpack lifted off

Pave Knife pod and two LGBs photographed on an F-4D of the 433rd TFS at Ubon on 12 May 1972. *(USAF)*

Wing CO Albert Piccirillo posing with his F-4's armament load. In this case there is a 600-gal centreline fuel tank, three CBU-24 anti-personnel bombs on the inboard wing rack and two LAU-3 2.75-in Folding Fin Aircraft Rocket (FFAR) launchers in pods holding 19 rounds each. *(Via R. L. Ward)*

at 08.20, following their chaff bombers which had launched on the hour. The four flights of F-4s used the codenames Jingle, Napkin, Biloxi and Goatee, the latter quartet carrying EOGBs while all the others were armed with 2,000 lb (907 kg) Mk 54 LGBs. Following aerial refuelling, the force located their chaff corridor on radar and proceeded within it. Captain Messett had had good cause to remember the last time he had approached the Paul Doumier bridge; a back-seater then, he had won the Silver Star for taking control of the Phantom when the Aircraft Commander was hit during the roll in on the target. Enemy AAA fire had come close enough to shatter the front canopy and disable the AC. Recovering, Messett released the bombs and in his words, 'Got the hell out of Dodge'.

Flying the Phantom from the back seat (a situation envisaged by the USAF when ordering the F-4), Messett carried out an emergency refuelling and made it back to Ubon. Understandably, he had 'a long unsettled grudge against that bridge'. Now, moving his element out four wingspans from each other, Messett went in. Maintaining the formation necessary to correctly set up the LGB laser basket, the flight followed others which had already made their attack. Several bombs impacted the bridge structure and others were guiding on to it. When Messett's flight leader dropped his bombs from around 14,000 ft (4,267 m), he followed suit. Flak and SAMs were heavy; it was subsequently found that the defenders had fired more than 160 SA-2s at the strike force. And they put up 41 MiGs. No US aircraft were lost, however.

The bridge was struck by a percentage of the 22 LGBs and seven EOGBs: twelve direct hits were confirmed, four had probably hit and thirteen had not been observed due to smoke and the heavy defences. But the reconnaissance photos showed that the bridge was unable to carry rail traffic, with one span out and several badly damaged. Mike Messett was among those who celebrated in the Ubon Officers Club that afternoon. The mission had been 'sweet revenge' for his earlier dramatic mission. One flight leader reported that the Wolfpack had left 'one severely smoking bridge' across the Red River.

Just to make sure that this vital target stayed out of action, the Wolfpack went back the following day. This time one flight of F-4s, confident that the miracle laser bombs could secure a coup de grâce, was all that was required. In fact Mike Messett who led the element briefed to attack the bridge while Captain Dave Smith, leading the other two, constituted the only US strike aircraft in Route Pack VI that afternoon. Smith took his Phantoms to the Back Mai command post just inside the southern outskirts of Hanoi. While they knew that they were the sole *strike* element in the Hanoi area, Messett and Smith expected to see the rest of the target support aircraft as they arrived. They were not there. The chaff corridor had been laid too early due to a mix up over target times, and the MiGCAP and Weasels had left, convinced that the Wolfpack strike was not coming . . . Messett had things pretty much to himself.

Badly damaged on the 13 May strike by the Wolfpack, the Dragon's Jaw was subsequently attacked by US Navy air. It was not in use by 24 October, when this photo was taken. *(USAF)*

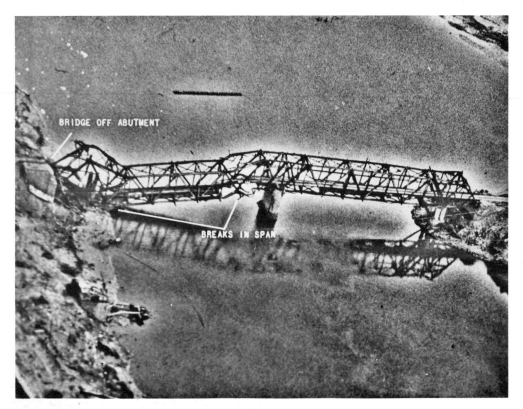

BRIDGE OFF ABUTMENT

BREAKS IN SPAN

The much-accursed Thanh Hoa bridge had in fact, finally succumbed to the 8th TFW LGB strike on 13 May. This is the post mission photo blow-up which confirmed what the crews thought they'd achieved during the attack. *(USAF)*

The North Vietnamese Fan Song radar watchers were also able to concentrate on the small force, not by this time hampered by ECM interference. A number of missiles were fired. Messett saw SAMs actually pass through the flight, but fail to detonate. He flew on. Two minutes passed before the bridge came into view, the Phantoms having streaked across Hanoi and turned for an easterly approach and roll in. The US pilots suddenly found they were not being fired at. Both SAMs and AAA ceased. Unhindered, the pilots released their weapons and left the area. Still the defences did not fire — it was a totally unreal situation.

Convinced his force had scored damaging hits, Messett awaited post strike confirmation. Eight LGBs, — six 2,000 lb Mk 84s and two M-118 3,000 pounders had been aimed at the bridge — and three more spans had been dropped. Three more were damaged.

Knowing the enemy's skill at repairing the irreparable, one more strike was planned for the Paul Doumier bridge. But not until 10 September was the weather good enough for LGB conditions. This attack put two more spans into the Red River and there was little evidence that much repair work had been attempted in the meantime.

Thus the USAF had achieved significant results against two of the highest-priority targets early in the Linebacker campaign — for on 13 May the Thanh Hoa bridge had been attacked again. The Wolfpack again sent out fourteen strike aircraft, heavily armed with a total of nine 3,000 lb (1,360 kg), fifteen 2,000 lb (907 kg) and 48 500 lb (227 kg) conventional bombs. This force again dropped all its ordnance squarely on target, the defences once more proving ineffectual.

Post-strike reconnaissance showed the western span of the bridge wrenched away from its forty foot (12 m) concrete abutment and the superstructure generally distorted so badly that no rail traffic could safely use it for many months.

By late May the USAF had denied thirteen of the most important bridges to the NVA war effort. Hanoi was effectively isolated both from its supply sources in China and from its customers in the south. The 8th Wing's use of guided bombs had been outstandingly successful.

As Linebacker I took an increasingly heavy toll on the North Vietnamese ability to sustain the invasion, the situation which had at first seemed very serious, began to stabilise. South Vietnam's air and ground forces rallied well and by June the land battle was seeing what Richard Nixon called 'a situation completely turned around'. In the field the NVA was subject to sustained attack from the air by both SVNAF and US air forces, which for once had a host of clearly defined targets, including NVA armour. Laser-guided ordnance played its part in defeating tanks, although the greater destruction was caused by conventional bombs. From 1 April to 15

On 23 May it was the turn of the Lanh Gia railroad bridge. Located 65 miles northeast of Hanoi, it was left in this condition after an F-4 strike. *(USAF)*

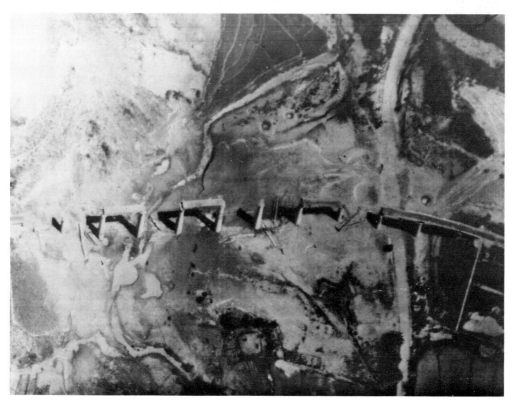

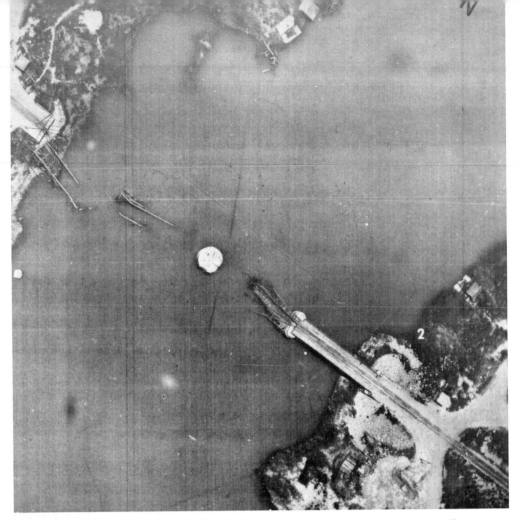

On 23 May 8th Wing Phantoms also knocked down the Bac Giang rail/road bridge. Three spans were dropped into the river and one supporting pier was collapsed. *(USAF)*

August, air attacks destroyed 285 NVA tanks in Military Region I alone.

Detection of well concealed armour proved difficult at times, however. The sharp eyes of the FAC continued to make a vital contribution. Equipped now with the rugged OV-10 Bronco, the FAC-coordinated attack could nevertheless destroy tanks in a phenomenally short time, as demonstrated on one attack that involved two 8th Wing F-4Ds.

The FAC found two NVA tanks north of a Marine position on the My Chahn river about a mile to the east of Route I. At twilight the Bronco pilot saw that a T-54 had got stuck in a dry stream bed and a PT-76 was doing its best to extricate it. Calling for ordnance the FAC, Lieutenant Colonel Ray Stratton, was told that none was immediately available. Finally two Ubon-based F-4s reached the area and set up their attack, having been briefed by Stratton on route. The FAC had also put down smoke markers. One of the F-4s carried the laser illuminator, the other two LGBs. Both aircraft were low on fuel so the attack had to be made without delay.

Sighting on the PT-76, the illuminator F-4 crew 'started the music' — meaning they had the laser beam on target — and the LGB-carrier released. The bomb blew the turret off and flipped the tank over. More music and a second run in. The result

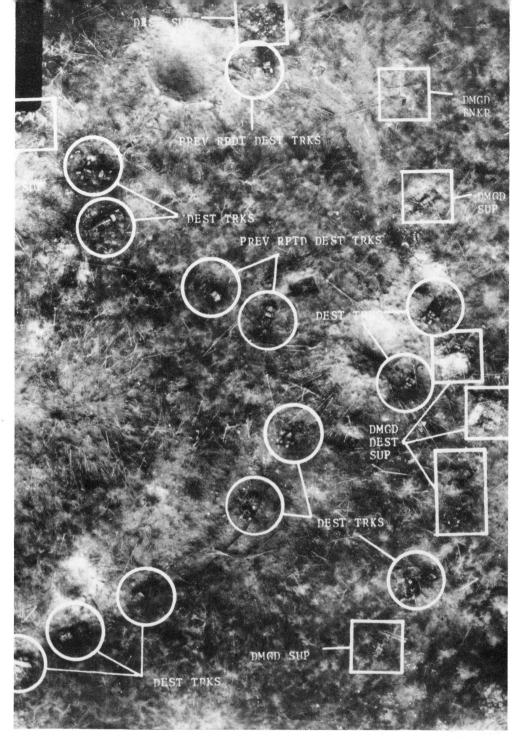

Throughout the war the US and South Vietnamese air forces conducted a massive campaign to stop NVA/Viet Cong supplies moving by truck down the Ho Chi Minh Trail. This post-strike photo records a successful attack which apparently caused 7,000 secondary explosions as the trucks succumbed to the rain of fire. *(USAF)*

was the same — two bombs to destroy two tanks within three minutes of each other. Stratton reckoned that had to be some kind of record . . .

The fighting continued through the summer months of 1972, the peace talks having resumed in Paris on 13 June. Some progress was made but still the North showed little sign of offering to withdraw or concede the right of the South to decide its own future. The bitter siege of An Loc showed that the South, well supported by US airpower, could fight tenaciously. In 1972 the Vietnam war literally 'came together', for there was a degree of military cooperation and coordination that had rarely been seen previously. The sophisticated, economical new generation of aerial weapons undoubtedly made a significant contribution, as did the fact that Vietnamese nationals, rather than the Americans, were doing most of the fighting. Equally significant was the fact that field commanders were making their own decisions on how given situations should be handled.

By integrating all aspects of airpower — FACs, strike, tactical B-52 sorties, air supply, rescue, medevac, Army helicopter gunships and Naval air strikes, dangerous situations could be dealt with very rapidly. Highly successful sorties by fixed-wing gunships added to the difficulties the enemy faced. It became clear that with total US dominance of the air, their cause was all but lost, at least militarily.

Politically, things moved painfully slowly and it was to be months before a breakthrough was achieved, only to be dashed at the eleventh hour, US problems being added to by the stance of South Vietnam's president Thieu. Not that the North had much to bargain with as time passed; their only card became the number of troops on the southern side of the DMZ — a force it proved impossible to dislodge.

Post strike evidence on 30 July 1972 of the 8th Wing's accuracy against the Canal des Rapides rail/road bridge. *(USAF)*

A November 1971 photograph showing a Loran-equipped F-4D loaded with LGBs keeping station with a fellow Wolfpack crew while a 432nd TRW Phantom, also with Loran, takes its fill from the tanker. Probably part of a small strike team, the three F-4s would join with the fourth element of the flight (almost certainly flown by the crew who took this picture) to answer a call to action, virtually anywhere in SE Asia. These three aircraft could bring gunfire, and highly accurate LGBs to bear on the target while *68-815* carries AIM-7s and a strike camera in one forward missile bay. *(USAF)*

Over North Vietnam itself, there came another round of air battles during the smaller, more precise 'surgical' strikes by the US as part of Linebacker I. Since the start of the campaign the USAF had, by 11 May, flown 1,800 sorties and shot down eleven MiGs for the loss of seven. But whereas before the 8th TFW had been in the thick of the clashes with the NVNAF, it had now largely handed over that aspect of the war to other Phantom wings.

Linebacker created widespread mission specialisation of aircrews, more so than had been possible during Rolling Thunder. The Wolfpack, concentrating on the precision delivery of munitions, became a crack air support force, its crews building a firm reputation through experience that was not to be diluted by other tasks. Combat air patrol became the province of the 432nd Tactical Reconnaissance Wing at Udorn. Having absorbed a number of F-4 squadrons, including the 555th Triple Nickel, the 432nd scored the lion's share of MiG kills for the remainder of the war.

Other specialised duty lay with Wild Weasel, anti-SAM and AAA strike squadrons and, as always, reconnaissance; in effect the Air Force had created a devastating 'strike package' able to undertake any kind of mission with virtually assured effectiveness. Despite the continued strength of the North Vietnamese defences, Linebacker forces were more able than ever before to contain and neutralise them, reducing losses significantly.

A typical strike package consisted of 32 F-4s carrying a mix of LGBs, EOGBs and conventional bombs, supported by twenty to forty aircraft to protect them. The latter would be one or two flights of F-4s configured for close escort, one flight of F-4 or F-105 Wild Weasels to seek out and destroy SAMs, a hunter-killer flight team of Thunderchiefs and Phantoms in the SAM and AAA suppression role and two flights of F-4s as the MiGCAP. Preceding each attack flight were one or two flights of A-7s or F-4s to lay the chaff corridor, these aircraft in turn having their own escort of F-4s, plus (if the target required it) their Wild Weasel escort and support. Finally a pair of RF-4Cs followed the strike force to photograph the target damage.

Other aircraft and ships provided stand-off ECM jamming and MiG warnings, the call signs Disco (for the EC-121 airborne early warning aircraft) and Red Crown (the US Navy control ship in the Gulf of Tonkin) being an integral part of the radio transmissions made during air strikes. Further jamming would be provided by the

The droop-nosed AVQ-10 Pave Knife laser designator pod was developed for use by the F-4D. It carried a low-light TV camera to serve a laser target illuminator. *(USAF)*

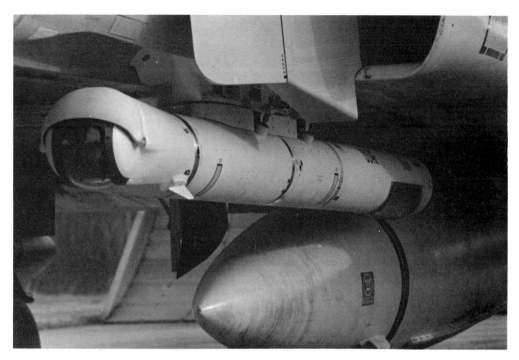

Also new was Pave Spike, the Westinghouse laser-seeker pod which was just one of a long line of 'Pave' equipments, the majority of which were the results of electronics-based programmes. *(USAF)*

trusty EB-66, and as always, the KC-135 tanker force would be on station to refuel any aircraft that reached bingo fuel state during the mission. Should a crew go down in an area where there was an even chance of rescue, a CH-53 Super Jolly Green Giant would be standing by. If the impending rescue bid was likely to be contested, an A-7 Sandy escort was also ready at short notice.

Although some well proven aspects of the air strike scenario had changed little, elements such as the chaff corridor and concurrent ECM 'pod formation' to blind SAM radars were new. That they were highly effective against the North's defence was well proven. Above all the USAF now had the technology to defeat new threats as they appeared.

# Chapter 14
# Last rounds

The last MiG kill credited to a Phantom crew flying with the Wolfpack occurred on 15 August 1972. The squadron was the 336th which brought the F-4E into the picture, although the regular squadrons of the wing remained with the F-4D for the duration of the Vietnam war. The 4th Wing's squadron was that day tasked with chaff dispensing and the succesful crew comprised Captains Fred W. Sheffler (AC) and Mark A. Massen (WSO). Sheffler's encounter report told the story of the engagement.

'Our mission was to provide support for two strike flights with laser-guided bombs against a thermal power plant and a railroad bridge along the north-west railroad at Viet Tri and Phu Tho respectively. We were the right outside aircraft in a formation of two flights of four. One minute prior to our first target our escort, the other flight, called a single bandit coming down from high six o'clock and attacking us on the right.

'Our flight began a hard turn to the right in an attempt to negate the enemy's attack. Escort told us that there were now two MiGs in the attack. We continued our turn, trying to visually pick up the MiGs. A camouflaged MiG-21 overshot at this time on my right, no further than one or two thousand feet [3-600 m] away. Captain Massen called for me to auto-acquire [pick up the MiG on radar rather than visually].

'I placed my pipper on the MiG and toggled the proper switch on my throttles. We achieved an immediate radar lock-on. I continued our turn to the right, striving to pick up the second MiG. Unable to achieve firing parameters, aircraft three gave me the lead, and at the same time Captain Massen cleared me to fire.

'I made a quick check to see if the MiG-21 was still at my twelve o'clock and then squeezed off an AIM-7 missile. By this time the MiG was about four to five thousand feet (1,200-1,524m) in front of me. For the next ten seconds, until missile impact, I divided my attention between monitoring the AIM-7's flight and checking our four to six o'clock for his partner.

'The missile made two minor corrections in flight; one just prior to impact on the left side, just forward of the tail section. He did not appear to take any evasive action up until the last second, when he hardened up his turn to the left. After impact and explosion, the MiG-21 entered a 45 degree dive, trailing smoke and flames from his aft section. I estimate his altitude when hit at between 9,000 and 10,000 feet MSL [2,740-3,050 m]. At this time the second MiG-21 came by on our

Publicity photo of the F-4E showing the M-61 gun and magazine, and Sparrow and Falcon AAMs. *(MCAIR)*

right in a hard left turn and went between our two flights head-on. We continued our turn and egressed the area at low altitude. Because of the ensuing engagement with the second MiG-21, I was unable to observe a 'chute or impact of the MiG-21 with the ground. However, the back-seater of an aircraft of the follow-on strike flight observed a large fire on the side of a hill near the area of the engagement during ingress, and it was still burning during his egress some fifteen minutes later.'

This victory in Route Pack VI was the fourteenth MiG-21 destroyed by an F-4 of the Wolfpack and brought the Wing's total kills to 38.5, 3.5 more than the total of the 432nd TRW. It maintained the 8th TFW's place at the top of the MiG-killing 'league table' for the USAF during the war.

Air combat victories during the Vietnam war were invariably hard-won, a fact reflected in the low number of aces compared with World War 2 or Korea: on 28 August Steve Ritchie became the first Air Force ace of the war, to be followed by Charles DeBellevue and Jeffrey Feinstein, with six and five kills respectively. Robin Olds just missed acehood with four kills; five F-4 crewmen scored three kills each, one had 2.5 and sixteen notched up doubles. With the exception of Captain Max Brestel, who gained both his victories at the controls of an F-105, all the double MiG victories went to Phantom crews.

Linebacker operations culminated in renewed results from the peace talks and the bombing pace was slackened until on 23 October all air operations north of the 20th parallel were halted. Henry Kissinger announced that 'peace is at hand'. Air operations continued in the south and the North Vietnamese position was for the

131

first time precarious. Nevertheless no satisfactory peace formulae could be agreed at that time and Nixon had little choice but to instigate Linebacker II on 18 December. The devastating precision bombing of Hanoi was an eleven-day campaign which all but ruined North Vietnam's ability to sustain the war.

Primarily the province of the B-52, the second Linebacker campaign again saw significant support from TAC strikes and it was not until early January 1973 before meaningful peace talks got underway again. Finally, on 27 January, the US underwrote an agreement to pull all its troops out of South Vietnam in return for North Vietnamese assurances that prisoners of war would be repatriated.

The war was far from over, however. Shifting its headquarters to Nakhon Phanom in Thailand, the US military command continued to direct missions until 15 August, the date of the last USAF strike mission of the war. This had been in support of the Cambodian government, then under threat from Khmer Rouge forces which had attacked the country earlier that year. But this effort was, like so many others during the SE Asian war, doomed to have little lasting effect as the US Congress finally vetoed any further expenditure for military operations in the region. Richard Nixon's Watergate crisis was also gathering momentum and

Close up view of the M-61 gun built into the F-4E, the kind of weapon Air Force crews had long wanted. In the event, F-4Es destroyed six MiGs with gunfire, one of which was helped in its demise by a Sidewinder. *(General Electric)*

Famed Phantom. Steve Ritchie's F-4D *66-7463* was still on the strength of the 432nd TRW at Clark AB in the Philippines in March 1974. This and other F-4s which had seen Vietnam combat continued to soldier on and many are still active today. *(D. Menard via George Pennick)*

media attention turned more to events at home than to the war which many Americans were already starting to forget.

The 8th TFW, which had been under the command of Colonel Carl S. Miller for most of the Linebacker I period, he having taken over on 28 February 1972, remained in Thailand until after the US pull-out. Command passed to Colonel Francis A Humphreys, Jr, on 25 November and he guided the Wing through its last phases of combat. The Wing operated over Laos until 22 February 1973 and was concerned with targets in Cambodia until 15 August. The augmented squadrons which had joined the Wing for Linebacker returned home in September, but it was mid-1974 before Ubon was slated for closure and aircraft, personnel and unit headquarters made preparations to leave. Final wind-down period was under the command of Colonel Tom M. Arnold, Jr, who took over the Wing on 25 January 1974.

The last scheduled training flight from Ubon took place on 16 July and on 16 September the Wolfpack had temporarily ceased to be. It moved without personnel or equipment to Kunsan, South Korea, where it absorbed the resources of the 3rd TFW which in turn had moved to the Philippines. In Korea, the task of the 8th TFW was primarily air defence. It continued to fly the F-4, maintaining air defence patrols in conjunction with ROKAF units, some of which were similarly equipped.

Korea has not been without tension in recent years and the Wing went on alert on 18 August 1976 following the killing of two US Army officers by North Koreans. As a precautionary measure, the Air Force augmented the Wing's squadrons by moving the 12th and 67th TFS from Kadena, Okinawa. The alert

133

Flying out of Kunsan, South Korea, on 5 March 1978 was F-4D *68-806* equipped with Loran and an AN/ALQ-119 ECM pod, to take part in Team Spirit 78, a joint US-Korean tactical exercise. *(USAF)*

period lasted until 8 September, when the augmentation squadrons were released.

It was fitting, in view of the Wolfpack's outstanding record in SE Asia, that five years after this incident (there have since been others) the Wing became the first overseas unit to receive the F-16. Decorated with an appropriate black wolf's head insignia, these aircraft brought single seat fighters back into 8th Wing service after a break of some seventeen years, the first Phantoms being exchanged for F-16As in September 1981. The Wing remains at Kunsan to the present day.

# Appendix 1
# Representative aircraft

| Sub-type | serial/tail code | Name | Squadron |
|----------|------------------|------|----------|
| F-4D | 66-7748/FG | | 433rd |
| F-4D | 65-725/FG | *Inferno* | 433rd |
| F-4D | 66-8239/FP | | 497th |
| F-4D | 66-724/FO | | 435th |
| F-4D | 66-7764/FO | *Ol' Eagle Eye* | 435th |
| F-4D | 66-8787/FA | | 25th |
| F-4D | 66-8777/FA | *Miss Magic* | 25th |
| F-4D | 66-8787/FA | *Dragon Wagon* | 25th |
| F-4D | 66-8782/FA | *Flave* | 25th |
| F-4D | 66-8784/FA | *Flipper of the Sky* | 25th |
| F-4D | 66-8794/FA | *Sour Kraut* | 25th |
| F-4C | 63-7683/FG | | 433rd |
| F-4D | 66-8796/FA | | 25th |
| F-4D | 66-8730/FP | | 497th |
| F-4D | 66-234/FO | | 435th |
| F-4D | 66-8817/FG | | 433rd |
| F-4D | 66-7583/FO | | 435th |
| F-4D | 66-8738/FP | | 497th |
| F-4D | 66-7596/HB | | 35th |
| F-4C | 63-7499/FG | | 433rd |
| F-4C | 64-848/FP | | 497th |
| F-4C | 64-829/FG | | 433rd |
| F-4D | 66-8761/FP | | 497th |
| F-4C | 63-7556/FG | | 433rd |
| F-4C | 64-708/FG | | 433rd |
| F-4C | 63-7668/FY | | |
| F-4D | 65-772/FA | | 25th |
| F-4D | 65-705/FG | | 433rd |
| F-4D | 66-234/FO | | 435th |

# Appendix 2
# Aerial victories credited to the 8th TFW

| Date | Enemy a/c type | USAF a/c type | Sqn | Callsign | Rank & Name | Crew pos | Credit |
|------|------|------|------|------|------|------|------|
| 23 Apr 66 | MiG-17 | F-4C | 555th | Unkn-04 | Capt Max F. Cameron | AC | 1.0 |
|  |  |  |  |  | 1/Lt Robert E. Evans | P | 1.0 |
| 23 Apr 66 | MiG-17 | F-4C | 555th | Unkn-03 | Capt Robert E. Blake | AC | 1.0 |
|  |  |  |  |  | 1/Lt S. W. George | P | 1.0 |
| 29 Apr 66 | MiG-17 | F-4C | 555th | Unkn | Capt William B. D. Dowell | AC | 1.0 |
|  |  |  |  |  | 1/Lt Halbert E. Gossard | P | 1.0 |
| 29 Apr 66 | MiG-17 | F-4C | 555th | Unkn-01 | Capt Larry R. Keith | AC | 1.0 |
|  |  |  |  |  | 1/Lt Robert A. Bleakley | P | 1.0 |
| 30 Apr 66 | MiG-17 | F-4C | 555th | Unkn-04 | Capt Lawrence H. Golberg | AC | 1.0 |
|  |  |  |  |  | 1/Lt Gerald D. Hardgrave | P | 1.0 |
| 16 Sept 66 | MiG-17 | F-4C | 555th | Unkn | 1/Lt Jerry W. Jameson | AC | 1.0 |
|  |  |  |  |  | 1/Lt Douglas B. Rose | P | 1.0 |
| 2 Jan 67 | MiG-21 | F-4C | 555th | Olds-01 | Col Robin Olds | AC | 1.0 |
|  |  |  |  |  | 1/Lt Charles C. Clifton | P | 1.0 |
| 2 Jan 67 | MiG-21 | F-4C | 555th | Olds-04 | Capt Walter S. Radeker III | AC | 1.0 |
|  |  |  |  |  | 1/Lt James E. Murray III | P | 1.0 |
| 2 Jan 67 | MiG-21 | F-4C | 555th | Ford-02 | Capt Everett T. Raspberry Jr | AC | 1.0 |
|  |  |  |  |  | 1/Lt Robert W. Western | P | 1.0 |
| 2 Jan 67 | MiG-21 | F-4C | 555th | Olds-02 | 1/Lt Ralph F. Wetterhahn | AC | 1.0 |
|  |  |  |  |  | 1/Lt Jerry K. Sharp | P | 1.0 |
| 2 Jan 67 | MiG-21 | F-4C | 433rd | Rambler-04 | Maj Philip P. Combies | AC | 1.0 |
|  |  |  |  |  | 1/Lt Lee R. Dutton | P | 1.0 |
| 2 Jan 67 | MiG-21 | F-4C | 433rd | Rambler-01 | Capt John B. Stone | AC | 1.0 |
|  |  |  |  |  | 1/Lt Clifton P. Dunnegan Jr | P | 1.0 |
| 2 Jan 67 | MiG-21 | F-4C | 433rd | Rambler-02 | 1/Lt Lawrence J. Glynn Jr | AC | 1.0 |
|  |  |  |  |  | 1/Lt Lawrence E. Cary | P | 1.0 |
| 6 Jan 67 | MiG-21 | F-4C | 555th | Crab-02 | Maj Thomas M Hirsch | AC | 1.0 |
|  |  |  |  |  | 1/Lt Roger J. Strasswimmer | P | 1.0 |
| 6 Jan 67 | MiG-21 | F-4C | 555th | Crab-01 | Capt Richard M. Pascoe | AC | 1.0 |
|  |  |  |  |  | 1/Lt Norman E. Wells | P | 1.0 |
| 4 May 67 | MiG-21 | F-4C | 555th | Flamingo-01 | Col Robin Olds | AC | 1.0 |
|  |  |  |  |  | 1/Lt William D. Lafever | P | 1.0 |
| 13 May 67 | MiG-17 | F-4C | 433rd | Harpoon-01 | Maj William L. Kirk | AC | 1.0 |
|  |  |  |  |  | 1/Lt Stephen A. Wayne | P | 1.0 |
| 13 May 67 | MiG-17 | F-4C | 433rd | Harpoon-03 | Lt Col Fred A Haeffner | AC | 1.0 |
|  |  |  |  |  | 1/Lt Michael R. Bever | P | 1.0 |

| Date | MiG | Aircraft | Unit | Call | Crew | Role | Credit |
|---|---|---|---|---|---|---|---|
| 20 May 67 | MiG-17 | F-4C | 433rd | Tampa-03 | Maj John R. Pardo | AC | 1.0 |
| | | | | | 1/Lt Stephen A. Wayne | P | 1.0 |
| 20 May 67 | MiG-17 | F-4C | 433rd | Tampa-01 | Col Robin Olds | AC | 1.0 |
| | | | | | 1/Lt Stephen B. Croker | P | 1.0 |
| 20 May 67 | MiG-17 | F-4C | 433rd | Tampa-01 | Col Robin Olds | AC | 1.0 |
| | | | | | 1/Lt Stephen B. Croker | P | 1.0 |
| 20 May 67 | MiG-17 | F-4C | 433rd | Ballot-01 | Maj Philip P. Combies | AC | 1.0 |
| | | | | | 1/Lt Daniel L. Lafferty | P | 1.0 |
| 5 June 67 | MiG-17 | F-4C | 555th | Chicago-02 | Maj Richard M. Pascoe | AC | 1.0 |
| | | | | | Capt Norman E. Wells | P | 1.0 |
| 5 June 67 | MiG-17 | F-4D | 555th | Drill-01 | Maj Everett T. Raspberry Jr | AC | 1.0 |
| | | | | | Capt Francis M. Gullick | P | 1.0 |
| 24 Oct 67 | MiG-21 | F-4D | 433rd | Buick-01 | Maj William L. Kirk | AC | 1.0 |
| | | | | | 1/Lt Theodore R. Bongartz | P | 1.0 |
| 26 Oct 67 | MiG-17 | F-4D | 555th | Ford-04 | Capt Larry D. Cobb | AC | 1.0 |
| | | | | | Capt Alan A. Lavoy | P | 1.0 |
| 26 Oct 67 | MiG-17 | F-4D | 555th | Ford-03 | Capt William S. Gordon III | AC | 1.0 |
| | | | | | 1/Lt James H. Monsees | P | 1.0 |
| 26 Oct 67 | MiG-17 | F-4D | 555th | Ford-01 | Capt John D. Logeman Jr | AC | 1.0 |
| | | | | | 1/Lt Frederick E. McCoy II | P | 1.0 |
| 6 Nov 67 | MiG-17 | F-4D | 435th | Sapphire-01 | Capt Darrell D. Simmonds | AC | 1.0 |
| | | | | | 1/Lt George H. McKinney Jr | P | 1.0 |
| 6 Nov 67 | Mig-17 | F-4D | 435th | Sapphire-01 | Capt Darrell D. Simmonds | AC | 1.0 |
| | | | | | 1/Lt George H. McKinney Jr | P | 1.0 |
| 19 Dec 67 | MiG-17 | F-4D | 435th | Nash-01 | Maj Joseph D. Moore | AC | 0.5 |
| | | | | | 1/Lt George H. McKinney Jr | P | 0.5 |
| | | F-105F | 333rd* | Otter-02 | Maj William M. Dalton | P | 0.5 |
| | | | | | Maj James L. Graham | EWO | 0.5 |
| 3 Jan 68 | MiG-17 | F-4D | 435th | Olds-01 | Lt Col Clayton K. Squier | AC | 1.0 |
| | | | | | 1/Lt Michael D. Muldoon | P | 1.0 |
| 3 Jan 68 | MiG-17 | F-4D | 433rd | Tampa-01 | Maj Bernard J. Bogoslofski | AC | 1.0 |
| | | | | | Capt Richard L. Huskey | P | 1.0 |
| 18 Jan 68 | MiG-17 | F-4D | 435th | Otter-01 | Maj Kenneth A. Simonet | AC | 1.0 |
| | | | | | 1/Lt Wayne O. Smith | P | 1.0 |
| 6 Feb 68 | MiG-21 | F-4D | 433rd | Buick-04 | Capt Robert H. Boles | AC | 1.0 |
| | | | | | 1/Lt Robert B. Battista | P | 1.0 |
| 12 Feb 68 | MiG-21 | F-4D | 435th | Buick-01 | Lt Col Alfred E. Lang Jr | AC | 1.0 |
| | | | | | 1/Lt Randy P. Moss | P | 1.0 |
| 14 Feb 68 | MiG-17 | F-4D | 435th | Killer-01 | Col David O. Williams Jr | AC | 1.0 |
| | | | | | 1/Lt James P. Feighny Jr | P | 1.0 |
| 14 Feb 68 | MiG-17 | F-4D | 555th | Nash-03 | Maj Rex D. Howerton | AC | 1.0 |
| | | | | | 1/Lt Ted L. Voigt II | P | 1.0 |
| 15 Aug 72 | MiG-21 | F-4E | 336th | Date-04 | Capt Fred W. Sheffler | AC | 1.0 |
| | | | | | Capt Mark A. Massen | P | 1.0 |

*355th TFW

# Glossary

| | |
|---|---|
| AAA | Anti-Aircraft Artillery |
| AAM | Air-to-Air Missile |
| AB | Air Base |
| AC | Aircraft Commander |
| ACT | Air Combat Tactics |
| AFB | Air Force Base |
| ARM | Anti-Radiation Missile |
| ASE | Airborne Support Equipment |
| CINCPAC | Commander-in-Chief, Pacific |
| CO | Commanding Officer |
| DMZ | De-Militarised Zone |
| ECM | Electronic Counter Measures |
| EOGB | Electro-Optical Guided Bomb(s) |
| FAC | Forward Air Control/Controller |
| FFAR | Folding Fin Aircraft Rocket |
| GCA | Ground Controlled Approach |
| GCI | Ground Controlled Interception |
| GIB | "Guy in Back" (slang for an F-4 Pilot or Weapons Systems Operator) |
| INS | Inertial Navigation System |
| LGB | Laser-Guided Bomb(s) |
| LGM | Laser-Guided Munition(s) |
| LOC | Line(s) of Communication |
| MiGCAP | MiG Combat Air Patrol |

| | |
|---|---|
| MIPR | Military Interdepartmental Purchase Request |
| MSL | Mean Sea Level |
| NVA | North Vietnamese Army |
| NVNAF | North Vietnamese Air Force |
| PACAF | Pacific Air Forces |
| POL | Petrol, Oil, Lubricants |
| PUC | Presidential Unit Citation |
| RESCAP | Rescue Combat Air Patrol |
| RHAW | Radar Homing And Warning |
| RIO | Radar Intercept Officer |
| ROKAF | Republic of Korea Air Force |
| RTAF | Royal Thai Air Force |
| SAC | Strategic Air Command |
| SAM | Surface-to-Air Missile |
| SOR | Specific Operational Requirement |
| SVNAF | South Vietnamese Air Force |
| TAC | Tactical Air Command |
| TDY | Temporary Duty |
| TFS | Tactical Fighter Squadron |
| TFW | Tactical Fighter Wing |
| TFX | Tactical Fighter, Experimental |
| USAF | United States Air Force |
| WSO | Weapons Systems Operator |